ASTROLOGY

A Guide to Understanding Your Birth Chart

YASMIN BOLAND

HAY HOUSE

Carlsbad, California • New York City • London
Sydney •Johannesburg • Vancouver • New Delhi

First published and distributed in the United Kingdom by:
Hay House UK Ltd, Astley House, 33 Notting Hill Gate, London W11 3JQ
Tel: +44 (0)20 3675 2450; Fax: +44 (0)20 3675 2451; www.hayhouse.co.uk

Published and distributed in the United States of America by:
Hay House Inc., PO Box 5100, Carlsbad, CA 92018-5100
Tel: (1) 760 431 7695 or (800) 654 5126; Fax: (1) 760 431 6948 or (800) 650 5115
www.hayhouse.com

Published and distributed in Australia by:
Hay House Australia Ltd, 18/36 Ralph St, Alexandria NSW 2015
Tel: (61) 2 9669 4299; Fax: (61) 2 9669 4144; www.hayhouse.com.au

Published and distributed in the Republic of South Africa by:
Hay House SA (Pty) Ltd, PO Box 990, Witkoppen 2068
info@hayhouse.co.za; www.hayhouse.co.za

Published and distributed in India by:
Hay House Publishers India, Muskaan Complex, Plot No.3, B-2,
Vasant Kunj, New Delhi 110 070
Tel: (91) 11 4176 1620; Fax: (91) 11 4176 1630; www.hayhouse.co.in

Distributed in Canada by:
Raincoast Books, 2440 Viking Way, Richmond, B.C. V6V 1N2
Tel: (1) 604 448 7100; Fax: (1) 604 270 7161; www.raincoast.com

Text © Yasmin Boland, 2016

The moral rights of the author have been asserted.

The information given in this book should not be treated as a substitute
for professional medical advice; always consult a medical practitioner. Any
use of information in this book is at the reader's discretion and risk. Neither
the author nor the publisher can be held responsible for any loss, claim
or damage arising out of the use, or misuse, of the suggestions made, the
failure to take medical advice or for any material on third party websites.

A catalogue record for this book is available from the British Library.

ISBN: 978-1-78180-647-0

Interior illustrations: 6 Shutterstock/ORLA;
all other images courtesy of the author

Printed and bound in Great Britain by TJ International Ltd, Padstow, Cornwall

MIX
Paper from
responsible sources
FSC® C013056

*This book is dedicated to my old
astro-colleague and pal,
the late, great Jonathan Cainer.*

Contents

Preface   xv

About the book   xix

PART I: THE BASICS OF ASTROLOGY

Chapter 1: What is astrology?   **3**

The origins of astrology   4

The zodiac   5

How does astrology work?   7

Branches of astrology   7

The birth chart, or horoscope   9

Chapter 2: Your birth chart – the map to your life   **11**

Casting your birth chart   11

Getting to know your birth chart   15

Identifying the zodiac signs in your chart   17

Identifying the planets in your chart   19

Identifying planets in signs in your chart   22

Identifying the houses in your chart   24

Identifying your houses' signs   25

Your ascendant, or Rising Sign   26

Chapter 3: Understanding the zodiac signs   **29**

The elements (Fire, Earth, Air and Water)   29

Fire, Earth, Air and Water signs   30

The elements in your chart   34

The qualities (Cardinal, Fixed and Mutable)   37

Cardinal, Fixed and Mutable signs   37

The qualities in your chart   38

The polarities (yang/yin)   41

The polarities in your chart   41

Chapter 4: Getting to know the planets   **45**

The inner and outer planets   45

Generational planets   47

The meaning of the planets   48

The Sun   49

The Moon   51

Mercury   53

Venus   55

Mars   57

Jupiter   59

Saturn   61

Uranus   63

Neptune   65

Pluto   67

The positive and negative sides of the planets   69

Chapter 5: Exploring the zodiac signs   **73**

The signs' ruling planets   74

The meaning of the signs   75

Aries   76

Taurus   77

Gemini

Cancer

Leo

Virgo 8ɔ

Libra 85

Scorpio 86

Sagittarius 87

Capricorn 89

Aquarius 90

Pisces 92

Chapter 6: The angles **95**

The ascendant (Rising Sign) 96

Signs on the ascendant 97

The descendant (the Love Line) 100

Signs on the descendant 102

The *Medium Coeli* (the MC, or Career Line) 103

Signs on the MC 103

The *Imum Coeli* (the IC, or Home Line) 105

Signs on the IC 105

Chapter 7: The houses **109**

Different ways of looking at your birth chart 110

Angular, succedent and cadent houses 113

House cusps 114

The meaning of the houses 116

1st house 118

2nd house 118

3rd house 119

4th house 119

5th house 120

6th house   121
7th house   121
8th house   122
9th house   123
10th house   123
11th house   124
12th house   125
A guide to your house rulers   125
Aries or Aries Rising   126
Taurus or Taurus Rising   127
Gemini or Gemini Rising   127
Cancer or Cancer Rising   128
Leo or Leo Rising   129
Virgo or Virgo Rising   130
Libra or Libra Rising   131
Scorpio or Scorpio Rising   132
Sagittarius or Sagittarius Rising   133
Capricorn or Capricorn Rising   134
Aquarius or Aquarius Rising   134
Pisces or Pisces Rising   135

PART II: GOING DEEPER

Chapter 8: Degrees, aspects and orbs   **141**
Identifying the degrees in your chart   141
Planetary aspects (aka planetary angles)   144
Conjunctions, sextiles, squares, trines and
      oppositions   145
The condition of a planet   148
Interpreting the aspects   150

Chapter 9: Aspect and chart patterns

Major aspect patterns   15

    The T-square   155

    The Grand Trine   156

    The Yod   158

    The Mystic Rectangle   159

    The Kite   160

Major chart patterns   161

    See-saw   161

    Tripod/splay   162

    Locomotive   162

    Bucket   163

    Bundle/wedge   164

    Splash   164

Chapter 10: Retrograde planets   167

What causes a retrograde?   167

How do planet retrogrades affect us?   168

The meaning of retrogrades   169

    Mercury retrograde   169

    Venus retrograde   170

    Mars retrograde   171

    Jupiter retrograde   172

    Saturn retrograde   172

    Uranus retrograde   173

    Neptune retrograde   174

    Pluto retrograde   174

The three passes of a retrograde   175

Chapter 11: The Moon's nodes   **181**

   Working with the Moon's nodes   182

   The meaning of the Moon's nodes   183

PART III: PUTTING IT ALL TOGETHER

Chapter 12: An introduction to chart reading   **189**

   Taking the birth chart as a whole   189

   Synthesizing a birth chart   191

Chapter 13: Your astrological cookbook   **195**

   Reading the planets by sign and house position   195

      The Sun   196

      The Moon   197

      The ascendant (Rising Sign)   204

      Mercury   205

      Venus   209

      Mars   212

      Jupiter   214

      Saturn   217

      Uranus   220

      Neptune   223

      Pluto   226

**Chapter 14: Love, money and other secrets
in your chart**   **231**

   Money   231

   Love   233

   Career, success and fame   235

   Lessons and luck   236

   Travel and adventure   237

   The way you come across to others   238

Family life	238
Children	239
Health	240
Sex	240
Creativity	241
Fears	241
Making friends	242
Life purpose	243
Chapter 15: Predictive astrology	**245**
What are predictions?	245
A note about the Astrological Cookbook	246
Making predictions with an ephemeris	247
Predicting with planetary cycles	254
Conclusion	257
Glossary	261
FAQs	268
Recommended reading	271
Acknowledgements	273
About the author	275

Preface

Astrology is a secret code to success. It's the most mysterious and enthralling subject I've ever come across – I've lived and loved astrology for almost 20 years now, and I'm still amazed by it.

Astrology is a divination method that's been tried and tested for millennia. I've used it to decode my own life, and to help other people in one-on-one consultations; I've also often employed it to help friends going through hard times. I've lectured on astrology in various parts of the world, had tons of positive live and digital feedback, held countless workshops, and written articles, columns and books about it.

I find it surprising – and somewhat infuriating – that some of the greatest scientific minds in the world today completely dismiss astrology, without having studied it, or tested it for five minutes, let alone the decades it takes to learn it properly. My first astrology teacher repeatedly told me to Test it! Test it! Test it! and I continue to test astrology every day of my life. The simple fact is: astrology works, and in this book, I will show you how.

My astrological beginnings

The friends I made in high school insist that I was very interested in astrology – talking about the stars and signs – way back then. I genuinely have no recollection of this, and my only early memory of astrology, from when I was about 12 years old, was reading my horoscope in a British teen magazine for girls called *Pink*. I lived in Tasmania, Australia, and wondered whether the information it contained was the same for the northern and southern hemispheres (it is).

As far as I'm concerned, my journey (in this lifetime) as a stargazer began back in my days as a freelance journalist. A friend who was a serious astrologer was clearing her office of astrology books in preparation for a move, and, knowing I was interested in the subject, she donated several boxes of her favourite titles to me. It was a true treasure trove and straight away I sensed that something big was happening.

Essentially, my friend gifted me with a handpicked collection of the very best astrology books of the previous 100 years or so, written by the most recognized authors. They were worth hundreds or even thousands of pounds, but beyond their material value, I knew instinctively they were going to change my life. When I look back on that gift, I feel it was karmic. That same friend also gave me some simple lessons in how to work out my birth chart and create charts for friends; she also briefed me on making predictions.

I started reading those astrology books, and compared what I found in them with my own chart. Suddenly, I made sense to myself! I think, with the exception of learning how to meditate, it was the most revelatory experience I've ever had. I believe that we incarnate with the birth chart we do because we have lessons to learn from what's in that birth chart. 'Decoding' that information is astrology's job, and here I was, being given the decoding keys.

Suffice it to say, I fell in love with astrology almost instantly. I delved into it more and more deeply every day: I couldn't stop reading those books. I also signed up to several online astrology lists, which allowed me to communicate with amazing astrologers across the world.

Looking back, I can hardly explain the rapture I felt as I learned about signs and planets and houses, and so much more. It was incredible. I discovered that everything you can imagine is covered in a birth chart, and it all fits together in quite a mind-blowing way. I went through my own chart – learning about which planet meant what, and why I was the way I was – and then I went through all my friends' charts and those of my colleagues and my exes. Suddenly, so much that had previously been a mystery was... *obvious!*

Today, when I meet someone who grabs my interest, I want to see their birth chart almost immediately – which is why I have astrology software in my phone! A birth chart tells us so much about a person, not least of which is where we are compatible with them, or where we might clash. Stories about a person's childhood and upbringing might speak volumes, but to an astrologer, that's nothing compared to seeing their horoscope!

My early, sudden immersion into astrology totally changed my life, and not just because it became my career. For one thing, it gave me a new framework to use. I remember one friend – Nicola, a very practical Capricorn – asking me in a slightly horrified voice, 'Do you actually make decisions based on astrology?' To which I muttered something like, 'Er, sort of, but I do also use logic!'

However, the truth is, I *do* base a lot of my decisions on the stars, and they have never let me down. When I met the man who would become my husband, Olivier, I had astrological software on my Palm Pilot, which I carried with me on our first date. As Olivier and I enjoyed our drinks, I managed to wangle his birth data out of him. When I saw his Moon was on my Venus, I knew I was onto something good!

I recently received a very pleasing email from a new friend, spiritual teacher George Lizos, whose birth chart I'd read for the first time. In it, he said something that really made my day: 'I honestly never thought that astrology could be so empowering. For a long time I thought of it as something that controls you and restricts you in some way, but now I understand how it really pushes you to grow.'

I was delighted by George's words because that's exactly how I see astrology – as something we can use to lift ourselves up! That's how astrology should be, and it's the astrology I hope you'll come to practise.

In this book, I hope to pass on to you my abiding passion and enthusiasm for astrology. If you try it and test it – on yourself and others – I'm sure you'll discover that it works like a charm. Join me now as we take a spin around the solar system.

About the book

Astrology is a hugely complex system, with texts, references, rules and techniques that date back thousands of years. It can take years, even decades, to acquire in-depth knowledge of astrology: I've been studying it for nearly two decades and I still consider myself a student. However, once you've learned the foundational principles and techniques of astrology – all of which are clearly explained in a simple, step-by-step way in this book – you'll have more than enough to start testing it right away.

This book will teach you everything you need to know to cast, understand and interpret your birth chart, and those of your friends, family members, lovers, potential lovers and anyone else whose time, date and place of birth you can get your hands on. You'll learn how to interpret the revealing personal data a birth chart contains and gain invaluable insights into why you do the things you do.

This book is organized into three parts, built around the four pillars of astrology: the planets, the signs of the zodiac, the houses, and the aspects. Once you have a good grasp of these, and how they relate to each other, you'll have cracked astrology's secret code.

Part I: This section explains how to cast your own birth chart online; you'll then refer to it as you read the book and complete some simple exercises. Here you'll learn about the elements – Fire, Earth, Air and Water – and about the Sun, Moon and planets: the main heavenly bodies most astrologers traditionally study. Understanding these, and locating them in your birth chart, is the first step towards being able to decode your horoscope. A birth chart is divided into sections – 12 houses, 12 cusps (the dividing line between the houses) and 4 angles. You'll learn all about these in Part I.

Part II: After learning about the planets, signs and houses, we take a look at the degrees and aspects – the connection, or relationships, between planets and other points in the birth chart, which alter the interpretation of the planets and signs involved. Having a basic understanding of degrees and aspects opens you up to real astrology that goes way beyond the Sun sign horoscopes you read in newspapers and magazines, which have their place, but are just the tip of the iceberg. You'll also learn about the various patterns that the distribution of the planets in a chart can make, and what they mean.

Part III This is where you start to learn how to put all that you've learned together. At this point you'll have identified the planets in your chart, and know which sign and house they are in, but how can you tell what all that means? This section contains what astrologers call a 'cookbook' – brief interpretations of what happens when you put a planet in a sign or a planet in a house. And for those of you who would like to go deeper in your studies, I've included a brief guide to making predictions.

Part I
THE BASICS OF ASTROLOGY

Chapter 1
What is astrology?

The word astrology comes from the early Latin word *astrologia*, which derives from the Greek word ἀστρολογία. When we break the latter down, we see ἄστρον – *astron*, or 'star' – and λογία – *logia*, or 'study of'. So astrology is 'the study of the stars'.

For millennia, astrologers have studied the movement of the planets around the Sun and against the backdrop of the fixed stars – as well as the movement of the Moon around the Earth – and have interpreted the interplay between the planets and our Earth. Astrology is therefore an investigation into how the positions and movements of the Sun, Moon, planets and fixed stars correlate with what's happening on Earth, and in our lives.

But do these heavenly cycles and cosmic events *cause* the events in our world, or do they merely *reflect* them? That's the million-dollar question. What I can tell you is that the so-called father of astrology, a possibly mythical figure called Hermes Trismegistus, is credited with summing up the idea of how astrology 'works', in a text known as the *Emerald Tablet*, with these words:

As below, so above
As above, so below
to accomplish the miracle of the One Thing

The origins of astrology

The first organized system of astrology was created in the 2nd millennium BCE by the Babylonian culture in Mesopotamia (a region in southwestern Asia where the world's earliest civilization developed). The Babylonians drew on their observations of the skies to create omens that were mainly used to predict the weather and political events.

But it has been argued that astrology may have begun much earlier than this: while humans were still living in caves. Markings on bones and on cave walls in France and elsewhere show that the Moon's cycles were being noted as early as 25,000 years ago. Early humans needed to understand nature and Earth's cycles in order to survive and thrive in time with the changing seasons. Following the lunar cycles made that a little bit easier to achieve.

Over thousands of years, legends and theories grew up around astrology. First, ordinary people, and then astrologers, started to ask questions about what they were seeing in the skies, such as: 'What's the overall theme of the events that occur on Earth when we see Venus near Jupiter?', 'What happens here when we see Mars opposite Saturn?', and 'What about the New Moon and the Full Moon? Do different things happen at these times?' The observations and interpretations made about these celestial events were tested and retested and found to be accurate.

In the earliest days of stargazing, all aspects of human life were believed to have a correspondence in one of the seven 'classical planets' – the Sun, the Moon, and the planets Mercury, Venus, Mars, Jupiter and Saturn. However, when the planets that modern astrologers now use – Uranus, Neptune and Pluto – were discovered, and incorporated into the existing astrological system, some of the planetary meanings shifted; for example, glamour moved from Venus to Neptune, and drugs from Mars to Neptune.

Acceptance by astrologers of the meanings and interpretations attributed to the modern planets was a slow process. Even today there are some working astrologers who refuse to use Uranus, Neptune and Pluto in their chart calculations and interpretations. However, the astrologers who do use them are now in agreement about their meanings, along with those of the classical planets. In this book, I'm using the modern system and including Uranus, Neptune and Pluto, not least because I believe that astrology evolves.

The zodiac

When studying the stars, astrologers essentially note the movement of the Sun, Moon and planets around the zodiac – an imaginary band in the sky around which the Sun passes in its apparent path across the Earth's sky. The zodiac is divided into 12 equal sections that are known by the names of the astrological signs: Aries, Taurus, Gemini, Cancer, Leo, Virgo, Libra, Scorpio, Sagittarius, Capricorn, Aquarius and Pisces. For each planetary placement – for example, when Venus moves through Gemini or Cancer or Leo – astrologers make different interpretations.

Because of the way the Earth wobbles on its axis, there's a shift in how we see the stars (a phenomenon known as the precession of the equinoxes). That means the constellations move one degree every 71.6 years, so the zodiac signs no longer correspond to the actual constellations. The signs are symbolic, but this is the system used by astrologers, and it works.

All the planets move around the Sun in one direction, taking varying lengths of time to complete an orbit. As they move about the 360 degrees of our skies, they make angles to each other; these angles – which are known as 'aspects' – are arguably the crux of astrology. You'll learn all about the significance of aspects in Chapter 8.

As an aside, although we often think of our solar system as a globe, it actually resembles a flat disc: this stylized illustration gives you an idea of what it looks like:

Figure 1: The solar system

How does astrology work?

No one really knows how astrology works. As I've explained, modern astrology emerged out of an ancient awareness that we're a microcosm of the universe, and I believe astrology works because we're all connected to all life everywhere. *Everything* is connected. The microcosm is in the macrocosm. Everything affects everything. Hermes Trismegistus's notion of *As above, so below* is central to astrology and reflects this idea.

We can think of the stars as a great cosmic 'clock'. For example, Saturn is traditionally interpreted as the sombre planet of the zodiac, so when the Saturn alarm bell rings on the great cosmic clock (in other words, when Saturn makes an angle, or aspect, to another planet), it's time to get serious. Mercury is the chatty planet of communications, among other things, so when the Mercury alarm bell rings, it's time to start communicating.

Essentially, astrology is mysterious. You could call it a secret of the heavens. You could call it a gift of knowledge, God/Goddess or the universe.

Branches of astrology

There are quite a few different types of astrology, but these are the two main branches:

Natal astrology – this is the study of the positions of the planets at the time of a person's birth. An astrologer draws up a circular 'map' of the sky at that precise moment, and this is called a birth chart or horoscope.

The astrologer then uses the horoscope to deduce the talents and challenges that individual will face in his or her lifetime. Essentially, natal astrology helps us to know and understand ourselves.

Predictive astrology – after a person is born, the planets obviously continue to change position. As they continue to move around the skies (which is called a transit), an astrologer will calculate how they move around that individual's birth chart and what angles they make to the other planets there. Using this information, they make predictions.

When I started to study astrology seriously, I was more interested in predictions than anything else. I thought, somewhat dismissively, that I already knew and understood myself. Today though, I value natal and predictive astrology equally, as both are so revelatory.

As well as these two main forms of astrology, there's also mundane astrology (the study of the effects of the astrological cycles on nations), electional astrology (in which an astrologer works out the best time for a person to do something, or not do something), horary astrology (where a chart is cast to answer a specific question), medical and psychological astrology, and more.

In this book, we'll be looking at natal astrology, which could also be called 'horoscopic astrology' or 'judicial astrology' as it interprets the horoscope – the astrological chart cast for a person's exact time, place and date of birth – but we'll also take a brief look at predictive astrology in the final chapter.

The birth chart, or horoscope

The main aim of this book is to help you understand and interpret your birth chart. So, what is a birth chart, exactly? To an astrologer, it's a map of your life.

On a practical level, it's an astrological chart that provides a snapshot of the planets at the moment you were born, set for the place where you were born. So imagine that, just as you were emerging from your mother's womb, someone went into a garden, lay down on their back and gazed up at the sky. Imagine they could see the Sun, Moon, Mercury, Venus, Mars, Jupiter, Saturn, Uranus, Neptune and Pluto and then drew a circle and plotted in the points in the sky where these planets were located.

Right there is your birth chart, your natal horoscope. The exact planetary placements in that chart will not be repeated for 26,000 years. Your birth chart shows you where your opportunities and challenges in life lie; it shows you what your most likely options are in the future, based on what's going on for you right now.

Once you're able to decode your birth chart – a skill that you'll learn, step by step, as you work your way through this book – you'll effectively have a map of your life. And to your friends' and lovers' lives too; and if you have them, to your children's lives.

On the following page is the chart for Hay House's illustrious (Libran) founder, Louise Hay. By the time you finish this book, you should be able to decode her chart. Don't look now, but we have decoded the basics for you on page 260.

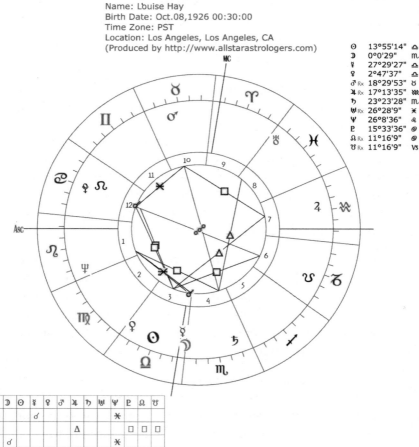

Name: Louise Hay
Birth Date: Oct.08,1926 00:30:00
Time Zone: PST
Location: Los Angeles, Los Angeles, CA
(Produced by http://www.allstarastrologers.com)

	☉	13°55'14"	♎
	☽	0°0'29"	♏
	☿	27°29'27"	♎
	♀	2°47'37"	♎
	♂ Rx	18°29'53"	♉
	♃ Rx	17°13'35"	♒
	♄	23°23'28"	♏
	♅ Rx	26°28'9"	♓
	♆	26°8'36"	♌
	♇	15°33'36"	♋
	☊ Rx	11°16'9"	♋
	☋ Rx	11°16'9"	♑

	☽	☉	☿	♀	♂	♃	♄	♅	♆	♇	☊	☋
☽			☌						✳			
☉						△				□	□	□
☿	☌								✳			
♀												
♂						□	☍			✳		
♃		△					□					
♄					☍			△	□			
♅						△						
♆	✳		✳			□						
♇		□		✳							☌	☍
☊		□								☌		
☋		□								☍		

Chapter 2

Your birth chart
– the map to your life

In this chapter you'll take the first giant leap on your astrological journey – by creating, or 'casting', your own birth chart (or horoscope) online. Then, as you read the subsequent chapters, you'll learn how to 'decode' the absolute *wealth* of personal information contained in your chart.

Casting your birth chart

The first thing you need to do is head to my website theastrologybook.com/freechart to cast your chart; once you're there, simply key in the time, date and place of your birth where shown, and your personalized chart will be automatically created. It's that simple. Enjoy the moment – it could be life-changing! (Note that for the most accurate chart, you'll need your *exact* birth time; if you don't yet know it, skip to the FAQs section below.)

Next, print out a copy of your birth chart, and take a moment to gaze at it. Just sit with it. On some level, you may well be remembering and recognizing it. As US astrologer Steven Forrest wrote in his book *The Inner Sky*, 'The birth chart is a blueprint for the happiest, most fulfilling, most spiritually creative path of growth available to the individual.' And now, that individual is you!

This could be a very important moment in your life. It's not an exaggeration to say that the information held in your birth chart could fill volumes of books. Your chart shows you the talents and challenges you were born with. It's a document that can reveal your life purpose, your likes, your dislikes, your fears, your abilities, the blessings you came down to Earth with, and the ways that you can surmount challenges. Contained within it is a guide to the obstacles you're going to face here on Earth, in this lifetime, in order for your soul to evolve. It can even tell you about your previous lifetimes.

Casting your birth chart FAQs

At this point in any student astrologer's journey, questions inevitably arise, so I've done my best to address some of them here.

What if I don't know the time of my birth?

There's no short and easy answer to this. The obvious thing to do first is talk to your parents, or perhaps an older sibling, and see what they can remember about your birth. No luck with that? Sometimes a hospital or birth certificate will contain the information you need.

Still no joy? If you're really determined, you can consult with an astrologer who specializes in ascertaining lost birth times, usually known as a rectification astrologer. He or she will note the big events in your life – the birth of your siblings, when you started school, when you graduated, started work, got your heart broken, got married or divorced and so on – and using that information, piece together the most likely time of your birth.

Alternatively, you can visit a kinesiologist, who will use a technique called muscle testing to tease out from you your exact time of birth. The idea is that on one level, somewhere deep down, you *know* the time of your birth, and this information is stored in your body and can be extracted using this particular method. Hey, you were there, right, so of course you know when you were born – deep down.

It can be fascinating to have a rectification astrologer work out your time of birth using traditional astrology methods, and then consult a kinesiologist to see what time your body 'says' you were born (obviously without revealing what the rectification astrologer has told you).

And if you don't want to go through all that rigmarole? Well, the easiest option is to use 6 a.m. as your time of birth when you cast your chart online. In doing this, your chart will be less accurate – you won't know your true ascendant, or Rising Sign, and you may end up with the wrong Moon sign (more on these later) – but as 6 a.m. is the arbitrary time that many astrologers use when the birth time is unknown, it's worth trying it. Others use midday. Better to have a less accurate chart than abandon your birth chart studies right here. Perhaps once you see how much information you can obtain even without knowing your precise birth time, you'll be tempted to dig deeper.

What if I was born by caesarean section?
Most astrologers, including me, believe we're born at the precise moment we're *meant* to be born. This applies whether you were born vaginally, before or after term, or by c-section at a time appointed by your mother (or by the doctor, who was playing golf that day and scheduled your arrival at x o'clock).

As smart as we humans are, I seriously doubt that we've worked out a way to change the very blueprint of our lives! So you have the chart you do because in it is a guide to all the lessons you need to learn in this lifetime and information about all the blessings coming your way – should you decide to live out the potential in your horoscope.

Do some people have 'better' charts than others?
No, they don't. Some people have 'easier' charts, though. For example, HRH Prince Charles has one of the 'easiest' charts you can imagine and his life has hardly been one long, terrible trial. But that's his karma – yes, karma is in the chart too (more on that later).

So if, after reading this book, you come to learn that you have a great chart or a troubled one, it's not about being doomed or blessed. It's about the lessons you need to learn in this lifetime. Astrological charts are neutral. Or as Shakespeare had it: 'there is nothing either good or bad, but thinking makes it so'.

A special note: You're about to discover how to know yourself by learning to read and interpret your birth chart – and in turn, those of your friends and family. You must pledge here and now to use wisely the information revealed in any birth chart.

So, let's get started...

Getting to know your birth chart

Astrology is underpinned by a system that more or less builds on itself, and each chapter in this book is designed to help you understand this system, layer by layer, and to see how it relates to your birth chart. Keep the printout of your chart to hand as you read on, so you can refer to it as you complete the simple *Take it back to your birth chart* exercises, which will guide you through all the new concepts and terms you're learning.

The layout

To begin with, you'll need to become familiar with the layout of your birth chart, and then identify the three most important astrological pillars or concepts on it: the signs of the zodiac, the planets and the houses. Let's start with the layout. You'll see that your chart is composed of several wheels within wheels – these might look complicated, even daunting, right now, but don't worry, before long they'll make complete sense to you.

Page 16 shows a blank birth chart on which the wheels have been labelled A, B, C and D – let's go through them in turn.

A. The central wheel – which on your chart contains small symbols and lines – refers to the connections between the various planets and other astrological 'points' in your chart (you'll learn about these connections later in the book).

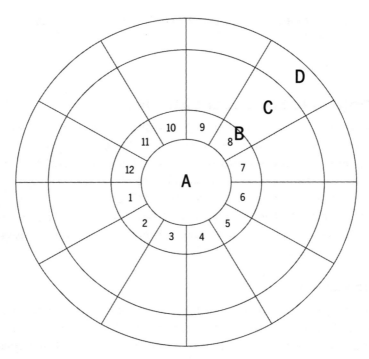

Figure 2: Birth chart layout

B. The next wheel out, a narrower one with sections numbered 1 to 12, divides the chart into what are called houses. These numbers denote the house numbers, so where it says 1, you have the 1st house. The houses run in an anticlockwise direction. House numbers won't always appear on your chart, but I've included them here for teaching purposes.

C. The 12 sections in this wheel are the 12 houses themselves.

D. The outermost wheel shows the division of the 12 signs of the zodiac, which run in an anticlockwise direction.

Identifying the zodiac signs in your chart

Let's move on to the 12 signs of the zodiac: the starting point for understanding astrology. You're probably aware that your 'personal zodiac sign' (i.e. whether you're a Gemini or a Leo or an Aquarius, and so on) is dictated by which zodiac sign the Sun was passing through on the day you were born; that sign is your Star sign, or as astrologers call it, your Sun sign. Below is a list of the zodiac signs in the traditional order used in astrology: the sooner you memorize the signs, *in the order shown here*, the better.

1.   Aries

2.   Taurus

3.   Gemini

4.   Cancer

5.   Leo

6.   Virgo

7.   Libra

8.   Scorpio

9.   Sagittarius

10. Capricorn

11. Aquarius

12. Pisces

However, you'll have noticed already that the zodiac signs on your birth chart (*see the outermost wheel – labelled D in the birth chart layout illustration above*) aren't indicated by their names, but by mysterious-looking symbols. For convenience, astrologers use symbols – which are known as glyphs – to represent the zodiac signs (and other information) on a birth chart. Believe it or not, once you get used to using glyphs, it's much easier than writing out the names for things in longhand.

Zodiac sign glyphs

Let's take a closer look at the zodiac glyphs: there's no need to memorize these just yet, but getting comfortable with them now will help your understanding. The table below shows the glyph and symbol used for each sign: the symbols give a good indication of the 'energy' of each sign (you'll learn more about what this means later in the book).

Sign	Glyph	Symbol
Aries	♈	The Ram
Taurus	♉	The Bull
Gemini	♊	The Twins
Cancer	♋	The Crab
Leo	♌	The Lion
Virgo	♍	The Virgin
Libra	♎	The Scales
Scorpio	♏	The Scorpion
Sagittarius	♐	The Centaur
Capricorn	♑	The Sea Goat
Aquarius	♒	The Water Bearer
Pisces	♓	The Two Fish

Take it back to your birth chart

On your chart, write the names of the zodiac signs next to their glyphs.

Hint: you'll find the signs in the outermost wheel of your chart and once you've identified one sign, they run in an anticlockwise direction in the following order: Aries, Taurus, Gemini, Cancer, Leo, Virgo, Libra, Scorpio, Sagittarius, Capricorn, Aquarius, Pisces.

Identifying the planets in your chart

Now let's turn our attention to some of the other strange squiggles you see on your chart: the ones found in the section labelled C on the *birth chart layout* illustration above, and shown in the *birth chart with planets* illustration below. Among these are representations of the 10 planets of astrology: the Sun, the Moon, Mercury, Venus, Mars, Jupiter, Saturn, Uranus, Neptune and Pluto. (For the record, astrologers are fully aware that the Sun and Moon are not planets but what is known as luminaries, or lights. For simplicity's sake, though, we often refer to them as planets.)

As you know, when you look at your birth chart, what you're seeing is a snapshot of the heavens at the moment you were born: all 10 planets are in there. But once again, astrologers don't use words to denote this information – as with the signs, the planets are shown as glyphs.

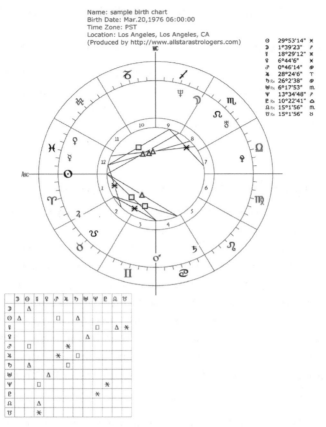

Figure 3: Birth chart with planets

Planetary glyphs

The table opposite shows the glyphs used to represent the planets on a birth chart. Take some time now to learn them. Try writing them out, and then see if you can name them. Then do the same in reverse. I've included some memory aids in the table to help you.

Planet	Glyph	Memory aid
Sun	☉	A circle with a spot inside it
Moon	☽	A crescent Moon
Mercury	☿	The winged messenger
Venus	♀	The symbol for femininity
Mars	♂	The symbol for masculinity
Jupiter	♃	The number 4 with a curl
Saturn	♄	A lower-case h with a cross through the top
Uranus	♅	A TV antenna
Neptune	♆	A trident
Pluto	♇ ♇	A crucible, or the combined initials 'PL'

The planetary glyphs have deeper meanings once you start to investigate them. Here is a brief outline of the glyphs' meanings:

❖ The Sun – spirit surrounds the seed of potential

❖ The Moon – a crescent Moon

❖ Mercury – shows Mercury's winged helmet and caduceus

❖ Venus – shows the Goddess's mirror

❖ Mars – shows a shield and sword, to fight in a battle

❖ Jupiter – shows Zeus's thunderbolt

❖ Saturn – depicts a sickle, akin to the image of death in medieval woodcuts

❖ Uranus – this is actually a stylized H, after Uranus's discoverer, William Herschel

❖ Neptune – depicts Neptune's trident

✦ Pluto – this planet has two glyphs (see table on page 21): the crucible, which is used on your chart and represents Pluto's Cap of Invisibility, and the combined initials 'PL', which are the initials of Pluto's discoverer, Percival Lowell.

Take it back to your birth chart

On your chart, write the names of the planets next to their glyphs.

Use the planetary glyphs table above as a guide.

Identifying planets in signs in your chart

So now you should be able to identify both the signs and the planets on your chart. Let's combine what you've learned so far and look at which signs in particular your planets are in. Start with your Sun. Find the Sun glyph on your chart. The section it's in will have a zodiac sign on its outermost wheel. If, say, the glyph for your Sun is in the section with the glyph for Aries on the outermost wheel, then your Sun is in Aries. Then look for your Moon: if your Moon is in the section with the Aquarius glyph on the outside, your Moon is in Aquarius, and so on.

Take it back to your birth chart

Make a note of the signs your planets are in.

On the printout of your chart, you'll find a list of your planets and which sign they are in. Using that and the information above, work your way around your chart and familiarize yourself with the location of your planets; record what you find here, or in a notebook.

For example:

My Sun is in Cancer

My Moon is in Pisces

My Mercury is in Gemini

Your turn...

My Sun is in _____

My Moon is in _____

My Mercury is in _____

My Venus is in _____

My Mars is in _____

My Jupiter is in _____

My Saturn is in _____

My Uranus is in _____

My Neptune is in _____

My Pluto is in _____

Do you see any 'double-ups' or 'triple-ups', or more? Is your Sun in one sign and nearly all your other planets in other signs? If that's the case, you might be one of those people who don't relate that strongly to their Sun sign. For example, if the Sun is the only planet you have in Leo, and you have quite a few other planets in neighbouring Virgo, you're probably going to think and feel way more like a Virgo than a Leo.

Identifying the houses in your chart

Next, you need to know some more basic information about the 12 houses. The houses you see on your chart are divisions of the ecliptic, which is the path the Sun appears to make across the sky from our point of view on Earth.

Take another look at the *birth chart layout* illustration on page 16. The sections labelled B and C show the house divisions: they look like this on your chart too. Note that the lines that divide each of the houses are called the house cusps (you'll learn more about these in Chapter 7).

The 12 houses

Each of the 12 astrological houses relates to a specific area of life. Here's a brief summary of what is governed by each house.

The 1st house: your appearance and image; self-identity; how you come across to others.

The 2nd house: cash, property and possessions; values, including how you value yourself.

The 3rd house: communications; siblings; neighbours; quick trips; early learning and education.

The 4th house: home and family, all things domestic; where you belong; your past.

The 5th house: romance; creativity; kids (your own or someone else's); pursuit of pleasure; love affairs.

The 6th house: daily routines, including at work; your health; duty.

The 7th house: your lovers, your spouse and your ex; open enemies; any sort of partner, including business partners; cooperation and competition.

The 8th house: joint finances; credit cards; debts; sex; anything you consider taboo; inheritance; transformation.

The 9th house: study; travel; the Great Cosmic Quest; the internet; higher learning; religion; spirituality; dreams.

The 10th house: your career and ambitions; how you make your mark on the world: what you're known for; your reputation.

The 11th house: friends; networks; social circles; hopes and wishes.

The 12th house: the deepest, darkest, most sensitive part of your chart. Your fears; your spirituality; self-undoing; withdrawal; secret or hidden enemies.

Identifying your houses' signs

The zodiac sign that's at the start of a house is said to 'rule' that house. For example, if you have Leo at 9 o'clock on your chart, then Leo rules your 1st house, and when it comes to 1st house matters (e.g. your appearance and how you come across to the world), you come across in Leo style.

Scorpio at 6 o'clock on your chart would be Scorpio ruling your 4th house, so when it comes to 4th house matters – such as home and family – your life has a Scorpio flavour. The house at 3 o'clock is your 7th house, so if you have Aquarius ruling your 7th house, in the 7th house matters of love and relationships you behave in a distinct Aquarian style. (You'll learn more about the meaning of the signs and houses later in the book.)

Take it back to your birth chart

Make a note of the sign that rules each of your houses.

Record this information here, or in a notebook.

The sign of _____ rules my 1st house

The sign of _____ rules my 2nd house

The sign of _____ rules my 3rd house

The sign of _____ rules my 4th house

The sign of _____ rules my 5th house

The sign of _____ rules my 6th house

The sign of _____ rules my 7th house

The sign of _____ rules my 8th house

The sign of _____ rules my 9th house

The sign of _____ rules my 10th house

The sign of _____ rules my 11th house

The sign of _____ rules my 12th house

Your ascendant, or Rising Sign

Even if you're new to astrology, you may have heard about your ascendant, also known as your Rising Sign. The Rising Sign is so-called because it's the sign that was rising in the

East at the moment, and in the place, you were born. To discover your Rising Sign, simply look at the sign that's at 9 o'clock on your chart, which is the sign on your 1st house. That sign is your Rising Sign, or ascendant. (Your Rising Sign is also shown on the list of planets on your chart.)

Take it back to your birth chart

Make a note of the sign your ascendant is in.

For example: My Rising Sign, or ascendant, is in Virgo

Your turn…

My Rising Sign, or ascendant, is in _____

SUMMARY

In this chapter, you've learned how to identify the three most important astrological building blocks on your birth chart: the signs, planets and houses. Now we're ready to go deeper, and to learn the significance of all this information.

Note that on your chart you'll also see two glyphs which look like ☊ and ☋. These are the Moon's nodes, and you'll learn more about them in Chapter 11.

Chapter 3
Understanding the zodiac signs

N ow let's look a little closer at the 12 signs of the zodiac. One of the most fascinating things about astrology is the fact that the signs have certain traits within them. You may already be aware that the signs are grouped into one of four elements – Fire, Earth, Air and Water – but they are categorized further. For example, Cancer is a Water sign but it's also what's known as a Cardinal sign and it's yin. Aries is a Fire sign and it's also a Cardinal sign and yang.

In fact, the 12 zodiac signs are classified in three different ways, into the elements, the qualities and the polarities. Essentially, these three classifications define the signs, and describe their fundamental characteristics. In the next few pages, you'll learn about the way the signs are classified – it's one of the details of astrology that makes the subject so deep, as no two signs are alike. We'll start with the simplest part of the system: the elements, also known as the triplicities.

The elements (Fire, Earth, Air and Water)
There are four elements, with three zodiac signs belonging to each element group. The elements are interchangeably

called 'triplicities' because there are three (triple) signs per element. The four elements are Fire, Earth, Air and Water.

The element that a zodiac sign is in reveals the sign's most basic temperament. Very broadly, Fire signs tend to be passionate, Earth people are more down-to-earth, Air people tend to live in their heads, and Water people are more emotional. Becoming familiar with the elements will give you massive insights into people's personalities and behaviour when you learn their Sun sign. The table below shows how the signs are grouped into each element.

Sign	Element
Aries	Fire
Taurus	Earth
Gemini	Air
Cancer	Water
Leo	Fire
Virgo	Earth
Libra	Air
Scorpio	Water
Sagittarius	Fire
Capricorn	Earth
Aquarius	Air
Pisces	Water

Fire, Earth, Air and Water signs

Let's now look at the element/sign groupings in more detail. You now know that the 12 signs are split into four categories – the elements of Fire, Earth, Air and Water. These overarching elements have particular characteristics. So even though Aries, Leo and Sagittarius are three very different signs, they have commonalities and a shared 'fiery' energy.

As you've seen, we all have all 12 signs of the zodiac in our birth chart: they run around its outermost wheel. The signs 'sit on' the 12 houses, which in turn are associated with every part of life you can think of. So it's definitely worth getting to know *all* the signs, even if you don't have any planets in a particular one.

A note about keywords: The descriptions of the element groupings below conclude with a few keywords that summarize each element. Keywords are crucial to astrology, and you'll come across them throughout this book. Start to take them in as you read on.

Fire signs – Aries, Leo and Sagittarius

These signs are the biggest livewires – the people who light up parties and turn heads. That's not to say we can't all shine like a Fire sign, but these guys more or less lay claim to that sort of behaviour. Even if your Sun sign is not a Fire sign, you have other planets in your chart, and at least some of these will have the highly creative Fire energy.

Aries, Leo and Sagittarius are different signs in one way, but all are fervent and hot-blooded. Wherever you have Fire in your birth chart – for example, a planet in a Fire sign or a Fire sign 'sitting on' one of your houses – you're likely to be anything but passive. Passions burn brightly in the Fire signs – and they burn hard and fast too.

Fire sign temperaments flare up but they can calm down just as quickly. A Fire sign in your chart is also where you'll go on some kind of quest or get 'fired up' with burning ambition. The fiery part of you is also the part that knows it can do anything; the part that's restless, always seeking and wanting to get things done quickly.

Keywords: fire; heat; burns you up!

Earth signs – Taurus, Virgo and Capricorn

These are the solid, strong and oh-so reliable signs. They are less bothered than the Fire signs about being flashy and getting everyone's attention. Earth signs are the down-to-earth people, and wherever you have Earth in your chart – for example, a planet in an Earth sign or an Earth sign 'sitting on' one of your houses – you're steady as a rock. Earth is the patient element that knows good things take time. Where you have Earth in your chart, and especially if your Sun is in an Earth sign, you know that slow and steady really will often win the race.

The Earth element is like the Earth itself: it nurtures, it's of service and it allows good things to come from its support. Think of our planet and all the life it supports, quietly and without asking for too much in return. That's the Earth energy. Earth is also very sensual, and even quite touchy-feely. Wherever you have an Earth sign in your chart (be it a planet in an Earth sign or an Earth sign 'on' one of your houses), you want things to be real and true and natural. Earth is also the element that refuses to be fake or false, even if the other elements want to show off or be indulgent.

Keywords: earthy words like earthiness; solid beneath your feet; helps you grow.

Air signs – Gemini, Libra and Aquarius
The element of Air is a little mysterious, just like the wind. People with a lot of Air in their chart (for example, a number of planets in Air) are harder to pin down. They can escape on the breeze. Air sign people are all about ideas – they love to talk and think and exchange ideas. They are in the realm of the intellect and that's where they're happy to stay. Somehow they seem less constrained by society's rules, and wherever you have an Air sign in your chart, you have this lighter energy. The element of Air is less about feelings.

That's one of the challenges of being an Air sign, or having a lot of Air energy in your chart (for example, if you have several planets in an Air sign or various Air signs): it gives you a wonderful lightness of being. However, you do need to anchor that energy too – make sure you're not being too hard to hold, or living too much in your head, wherever you have Air in your chart. The Air signs are very entertaining people and this is an element of wit, as well. Air signs don't really have that sharp edge. Or do they? Sometimes Air's rationality and pragmatism cut deep!

Keywords: airy things like thoughts, and tripping lightly, and chatter and ephemerality.

Water signs – Cancer, Scorpio and Pisces
This is the emotional element, the dreamy element. Water signs can *feel* their feelings – and how! You can't ask a Water sign how they're feeling and not expect an answer that touches you quite deeply: at least most of the time. Wherever you have a Water sign in your chart – for example,

a planet in a Water sign or a Water sign 'on' one of your houses – you're going to feel things really deeply, perhaps be elusive at times, be more in touch with your emotions, and generally emote a lot more.

These are three of the more retiring signs of the zodiac, and Water people are sometimes that, too. They are not necessarily the first people we notice at a party, but they could well end up being the ones we talk to most deeply.

There's a protective element to this sign too: it can be stronger than you think. The element of Water will do all it can to see off any threats to itself or anything it loves. Water is more sentimental and softer than the other elements. Water sign people are not pushovers – far from it – but there's a definite softness to them, at least around the edges.

Keywords: water and being fluid; emotions and dreams; soft, but sometimes rough

The elements in your chart

In Chapter 2 you worked out which signs your planets are in; next, you need to look at whether those signs/planets are Fire, Earth, Air or Water. Do you have a lot of Fire energy in your chart, or not much? Do you have a lot of Water in your chart? Air? Earth? Complete the following exercise to find out which, if any, element predominates in your chart.

Take it back to your birth chart

Discover which element is strongest in your chart.

To do this, you can simply calculate the number of planets you have in each element, or use what's called the points system, which astrologers prefer because it better reflects how influential certain planets and other points are in your chart. The more 'personal' planets (and other points) on your chart – i.e. the Sun, the Moon and the ascendant – are given 2 points, whereas the other planets are given just 1.

For example:

My Sun is in Leo – Fire [2 points]

My Moon is in Aquarius – Air [2 points]

My ascendant is in Virgo – Earth [2 points]

My Mercury is in Leo – Fire [1 point]

My Venus is in Virgo – Earth [1 point]

My Mars is in Taurus – Earth [1 point]

My Jupiter is in Aquarius – Air [1 point]

My Saturn is in Cancer – Water [1 point]

My Uranus is in Libra – Air [1 point]

My Neptune is in Sagittarius – Fire [1 point]

My Pluto is in Libra – Air [1 point]

I have:

2 planets + ascendant in Earth

4 planets in Air

1 planet in Water

Or using the points system:

    Fire = 4 points
    Earth = 4 points
    Air = 5 points
    Water = 1 point

Your turn...

    My Sun is in _____ [2 points]

    My Moon is in _____ [2 points]

    My ascendant is in _____ [2 points]

    My Mercury is in _____ [1 point]

    My Venus is in _____ [1 point]

    My Mars is in _____ [1 point]

    My Jupiter is in _____ [1 point]

    My Saturn is in _____ [1 point]

    My Uranus is in _____ [1 point]

    My Neptune is in _____ [1 point]

    My Pluto is in _____ [1 point]

So what have you found? Do you have more of one element than another? Make a note of how many planets you have in each element, to see which element is strongest in you.

    I have _____ planets in Fire [X point(s)]

    I have _____ planets in Earth [X point(s)]

    I have _____ planets in Air [X point(s)]

    I have _____ planets in Water [X point(s)]

The qualities (Cardinal, Fixed and Mutable)

Next, the 12 signs are divided into three groups containing four signs each. Each four-sign group is called a quadruplicity (also known as modes or modalities), and each of these quadruplicities denotes a quality. The three qualities are Cardinal, Fixed and Mutable. The qualities sort the signs almost into personality types. Understanding them is really worthwhile, and I recommend you memorize them as soon as possible. The table below shows how each sign is grouped.

Sign	Quality
Aries	Cardinal
Taurus	Fixed
Gemini	Mutable
Cancer	Cardinal
Leo	Fixed
Virgo	Mutable
Libra	Cardinal
Scorpio	Fixed
Sagittarius	Mutable
Capricorn	Cardinal
Aquarius	Fixed
Pisces	Mutable

Cardinal, Fixed and Mutable signs

Here is a very brief overview of the Cardinal, Fixed and Mutable signs.

Cardinal signs

The Cardinal signs are great at starting things, and they are the leaders of most packs. These signs also correspond with the beginning of nature's seasons.

Keywords: leading, initiating, assertive (also known as bossy)

Fixed signs

The Fixed signs are the ones with staying power, who also have a tendency to be, well, fixed!

Keywords: staying, enduring, patient (also known as stubborn)

Mutable signs

These people go with the flow but sometimes have problems finishing things off.

Keywords: following, meandering, adaptable (also known as easily led)

Take a moment now to think about yourself and the people you know well and consider how much you can see your own/their character in the quadruplicities of your/their Sun sign. Now imagine what happens when you get two people of the same quadruplicity in a relationship. In my family, for example, we have three Cardinal Sun signs and, yes, we all want to be the boss! Luckily, we have other planets in our charts which weave and merge more harmoniously.

The qualities in your chart

So now it's time to work out which qualities, or quadruplicities, you have in your chart – in other words, which planets are in which quality, and which quality predominates.

Take it back to your birth chart

Discover which quality is strongest in your chart.

To do this, you can simply calculate the number of planets you have in each quality, or use the points system. In the latter, the Sun, Moon and ascendant are given 2 points and the other planets 1.

For example:

> My Sun is in Leo – Fixed [2 points]
>
> My Moon is in Aquarius – Fixed [2 points]
>
> My ascendant is in Virgo – Mutable [2 points]
>
> My Mercury is in Leo – Fixed [1 point]
>
> My Venus is in Virgo – Mutable [1 point]
>
> My Mars is in Taurus – Fixed [1 point]
>
> My Jupiter is in Aquarius – Fixed [1 point]
>
> My Saturn is in Cancer – Cardinal [1 point]
>
> My Uranus is in Libra – Cardinal [1 point]
>
> My Neptune is in Sagittarius – Mutable [1 point]
>
> My Pluto is in Libra – Cardinal [1 point]

I have:

> 3 planets in Cardinal signs
>
> 5 planets in Fixed signs
>
> 2 planets + ascendant in Mutable signs

Or using the points system:

Cardinal = 3 points

Fixed = 7 points

Mutable = 4 points

Your turn...

My Sun is in _____ [2 points]

My Moon is in _____ [2 points]

My ascendant is in _____ [2 points]

My Mercury is in _____ [1 point]

My Venus is in _____ [1 point]

My Mars is in _____ [1 point]

My Jupiter is in _____ [1 point]

My Saturn is in _____ [1 point]

My Uranus is in _____ [1 point]

My Neptune is in _____ [1 point]

My Pluto is in _____ [1 point]

So what have you found? Do you have more of one quality than another? Make a note of how many planets you have in each quality, to discover which one is strongest in you:

I have _____ Cardinal planets [X points]

I have _____ Fixed planets [X points]

I have _____ Mutable planets [X points]

The polarities (yang/yin)

The final part of the classification system of the 12 signs we're going to delve into is the polarities – more commonly known as yang/yin.

❖ Fire and Air signs are known as positive, or yang

❖ Earth and Water signs are known as negative, or yin.

The polarities in your chart

These classifications are not a judgement that positive is better than negative, though; rather, the positive signs are the outgoing, seeking, more masculine energies while the negative signs are more inward-looking, and arguably more gentle and feminine. The positive signs seek and find while the negative signs attract and receive. (If you want to avoid using positive/negative for yang and yin, you can call them extroverted/introspective.)

Complete the following exercise to discover the balance of the polarities in your chart.

Take it back to your birth chart

Discover which polarity is strongest in your chart.

To do this, you can simply calculate the number of planets you have in each polarity, or use the points system. In the latter, the Sun, Moon and ascendant are given 2 points and the other planets 1.

For example:

My Sun is in Leo – yang [2 points]

My Moon is in Aquarius – yang [2 points]

My ascendant is in Virgo – yin [2 points]

My Mercury is in Leo – yang [1 point]

My Venus is in Virgo – yin [1 point]

My Mars is in Taurus – yang [1 point]

My Jupiter is in Aquarius – yang [1 point]

My Saturn is in Cancer – yin [1 point]

My Uranus is in Libra – yang [1 point]

My Neptune is in Sagittarius – yang [1 point]

My Pluto is in Libra – yang [1 point]

I have:

2 planets + ascendant in yin signs

8 planets in yang signs

Or using the points system:

Yin planets = 10 points

Yang planets = 4 points

Your turn...

My Sun is in _____ [2 points]

My Moon is in _____ [2 points]

My ascendant is in _____ [2 points]

My Mercury is in _____ [1 point]

My Venus is in _____ [1 point]

My Mars is in _____ [1 point]

My Jupiter is in _____ [1 point]

My Saturn is in _____ [1 point]

My Uranus is in _____ [1 point]

My Neptune is in _____ [1 point]

My Pluto is in _____ [1 point]

So what have you found? Do you have more of one quality than another? Make a note of how many planets you have in each quality, to discover which one is strongest in you:

I have _____ yin planets [X points]

I have _____ yang planets [X points]

The table below summarizes all parts of the classification system of the 12 signs.

Sign	Element	Quality	Polarity
Aries	Fire	Cardinal	Yang (positive)
Taurus	Earth	Fixed	Yin (negative)
Gemini	Air	Mutable	Yang (positive)
Cancer	Water	Cardinal	Yin (negative)
Leo	Fire	Fixed	Yang (positive)
Virgo	Earth	Mutable	Yin (negative)
Libra	Air	Cardinal	Yang (positive)
Scorpio	Water	Fixed	Yin (negative)
Sagittarius	Fire	Mutable	Yang (positive)
Capricorn	Earth	Cardinal	Yin (negative)
Aquarius	Air	Fixed	Yang (positive)
Pisces	Water	Mutable	Yin (negative)

Alternatively, here is a pictorial representation of the system of this information.

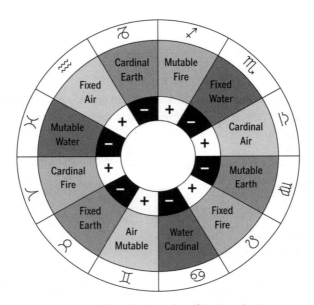

Figure 4: The 12 signs classification chart

SUMMARY

In this chapter, you've learned more about the characteristics of the zodiac signs. I hope you can already see that astrology is a far deeper subject than you might have expected. The astrological signs are not just a simple, one-dimensional concept; rather, within each are sub-classifications that define them in great detail – the elements (Fire, Earth, Air and Water), the qualities (Cardinal, Fixed and Mutable) and the polarities (yin and yang).

No sign has exactly the same element/quality/polarity grouping as another, so each sign is therefore a unique combination and expression of its element, quality and polarity.

Chapter 4

Getting to know the planets

So far, you've learned how to read the glyphs for the 10 planets of astrology, and then used these to discover the location of the planets on your birth chart. You also know which zodiac sign each of your planets is in, as well as the element it's in, its quality and its polarity. Now you're going to find out more about the planets themselves. On your chart, the planets are like 'characters', and they bring it to life.

The inner and outer planets

The word planet means 'wanderer', and indeed the planets are ever-moving. They revolve around the Sun and as they do so, they travel through the 12 signs of the zodiac. They do this at very different, and entirely predictable, speeds.

❖ **The inner planets** – the Sun, Moon, Mercury, Mars and Venus – move quickly around the chart, so you may well have these planets in totally different signs to someone born just a few days before or after you.

❖ **The outer planets** – Jupiter, Saturn, Neptune, Uranus and Pluto – move far more slowly (see the list below).

So, for example, anyone born within two years of you may well have Saturn in the same sign as you. (Note that although astronomers have recently diminished Pluto's status to 'dwarf planet', astrologers still treat it as a proper planet.)

Here's an indication of the length of time each planet takes to travel through the zodiac:

The Sun – one year

The Moon – 27⅓ days

Mercury – a rotational cycle of around 88 days. Note that because of retrograde motion (retrogrades are explained in Chapter 10), Mercury takes about a year to travel around the zodiac. It's in a sign for between 14 and 30 days. Mercury is never more than 28 degrees from the Sun.

Venus – a rotational cycle of around 225 days. Venus is retrograde every 18 months or so, and therefore takes about a year to traverse the zodiac. Note that Venus is never more than 48 degrees from the Sun.

Mars – a rotational cycle of around 687 days. Mars stays in each sign for about two months, except when retrograde (see Chapter 10).

Jupiter – around 12 years

Saturn – around 29 years

Uranus – around 84 years

Neptune – around 165 years

Pluto – around 248 years

Note that it actually takes 26,000 years for all the planets to be back in the same relationship that they were on any previous date. So, with the exception of people born within a few minutes of you in the exact same place, no one will have exactly the same chart as you for another 26,000 years. Where the planets were when you were born forms your horoscope chart, and the personality, assets and challenges with which you came into the world.

In astrology, the planets represent different parts of you. So, for example, your Sun is the part of you that likes to shine and show off, while Venus is the part of you that loves and spends, and Mars is the part of you that argues.

Generational planets

As you can see, Uranus, Neptune and Pluto are all very slow-moving planets – Pluto, for example, stays in each sign for between 14 and 30 years. These planets therefore shape entire generations of people, and as a result, they are often called 'generational planets'. For example, we speak of the Pluto in Leo generation (1939 to 1957) who brought us rock and roll and peaceful protests.

Generational planets is a subject you can explore further if you decide to delve deeper into astrology, but in a nutshell, and to reiterate the point made above, the faster-moving inner planets in a birth chart vary from one person to the next, even if they were born just a few days or weeks apart, whereas the slower-moving generational planets define generations, as they change signs far less frequently.

For example, you could have the Sun in Aquarius, Mercury in Pisces and Venus in Capricorn, and a friend born a few weeks after you could have a Pisces Sun and Mercury and Venus in Aries, but you both may have Saturn, Uranus, Neptune and Pluto in the same sign. Neptune, say, takes 165 years to go around the zodiac – so the chances are high that someone born within the same five or 10 years as you will have Neptune in the same sign (and thus element) as you.

Seeing stars

If you're lucky enough to live in a place where it's dark enough at night to see the sky properly, embrace it. Go outside and take a look at the stars and the planets. You can see Mercury, Venus, Mars, Jupiter and Saturn with the naked eye. The stars twinkle, the planets don't really. Better still, visit an observatory and check out the planets through a powerful telescope. There are also some excellent apps around (among them Starwalk) that will identify the planets when you hold your phone up to the sky.

When you start practising astrology, it's all too easy for the planets to become almost purely theoretical symbols you read without ever lifting your eyes heavenwards. I highly recommend getting outside at night, seeing what you can see, and also just feeling the wonder at having the heavens beaming down on you. As you probably know, we are all made of stardust! I would also highly recommend doing a basic astronomy course, if you get really serious about astrology. You'll find it highly useful.

The meaning of the planets

What follows is a description of the general characteristics and traits of the 10 planets used in modern astrology – those we're working with in this book as we decode your chart. After you've read and digested each planet's description, grab the printout of your birth chart and follow the instructions in the *Take it back to your birth chart* exercises.

Note that once again we're using keywords, this time for the planets. Start to get a feel for these as you read on, and try to memorize them. The keywords remind you of what a planet 'does' or represents in your chart. For example, Mercury is the communications planet and is about how we talk and listen, while Venus is the love planet and shows us how we love, and so on.

Each planet also has positive and negative expressions. For example, the Sun is all about confidence, so if we're in a positive state of mind and living our best life (i.e. 'living positively'), we'll shine brightly, but if we're in a negative state of mind (i.e. 'living negatively'), that confidence can topple over into arrogance. *Note that some of the keywords will make more sense once you start to work more deeply with astrology and start to make predictions.*

The Sun ☉

Living positively: The self; self-image; willpower

Living negatively: Ego; vanity; selfishness

This is what dictates your Star (Sun) sign. Your Sun is the essential you – your Self. It represents your ego. It shows your levels of confidence and where your focus is, in this lifetime. The Sun is in many ways the driving force in your chart. It's the centre of the planetary system: the giver of light and life. It's heroic and it likes to take centre stage.

Wherever the Sun is in your chart – in a particular sign and house – tells you a lot about what you came to do, here on planet Earth. It also tells you how and where you shine. As you discover more about your Sun, you'll discover more about yourself! It also tells you a lot about your likely central concerns.

Where's your Sun?
Earlier, you located the Sun in your chart, and made a note of which element it was in. In other words, you worked out if your Sun is in a Fire sign (Aries, Leo or Sagittarius), an Earth sign (Taurus, Virgo or Capricorn), an Air sign (Gemini, Libra or Aquarius) or a Water sign (Cancer, Scorpio or Pisces). Below is a brief overview of what it means to have your Sun in a particular element.

❖ **Fire sign**: you're more likely to be fiery! Fire sign folk are full of va va voom.

❖ **Earth sign**: you're more likely to be quite down-to-earth.

❖ **Air sign**: you're more than likely to live in your head rather than your heart.

❖ **Water sign**: you're one of the more emotional types around – sentimental and possibly clingy.

If all you know about a person is their Sun sign, you already know a lot about them because the Sun is their focus in this lifetime. That's one of the many reasons why the Sun sign, or house, astrology you read in newspapers and magazines works – because the Sun is such a crucial and central part of the birth chart. If you want to know your life purpose, your Sun is one of the pointers in your chart. It tells you a lot about who you really are.

Keywords for what the Sun represents: who you really are; where you shine; where your focus is in this lifetime; your individuality; how bold you are; your male/yang side.

For an interpretation of the Sun in each sign, go to page 75 and read up on the main characteristics of each sign. Your Sun will exude the character of its zodiac sign.

Take it back to your birth chart

On your chart, draw an arrow pointing to the Sun glyph, and beside it, write the words 'Who I really am.'

The Moon ☾

Living positively: Feeling; nurturing; instincts

Living negatively: Neediness; moodiness; timidity

Most people know their Sun sign, but that's about where it ends. Yet knowing your own or someone else's Moon sign gives you massive insights into yourself and them. The Moon is about our inner nature. In your chart, it tells you what you *need*. And once you know that, you can set about getting it, right?

If you look at the Moon sign and house of someone you know well, you'll instantly understand more about what they need. Can you provide it? The Moon in your chart can also tell you about your home, how you grew up, how things were with your mother, about what feeds you, about your feelings, your unconscious, and your instincts.

The Moon's sign and house will reveal your sympathies and imaginings. What makes you feel secure? Once you understand your Moon, you'll better understand your own needs. The Moon is mysterious and even occult-ish. It also rules receptivity, fertility, femininity, the Goddess, cycles and moods. This planet changes more frequently than any of the main heavenly bodies we'll be looking at.

Where's your Moon?
Is your Moon in a Fire sign (Aries, Leo or Sagittarius), an Earth sign (Taurus, Virgo or Capricorn), a Water sign (Cancer, Scorpio or Pisces) or an Air sign (Gemini, Libra or Aquarius)? Below is a brief overview of what it means to have your Moon in a particular element:

❖ **Fire sign**: you have fiery emotions.

❖ **Earth sign**: you're emotionally steadfast.

❖ **Air sign**: you may need to work harder to connect with your emotions.

❖ **Water sign**: you're very emotional.

Keywords for what the Moon represents: what you need; what feeds you; your relationship with your mother; your yin/feminine side; your feelings; how sensitive you are; how intuitive you are; your instincts; your emotional security (or lack of); your subconscious, memory and imagination; your protective maternal side, domesticity.

Interpretations for the Moon in each sign and house of the birth chart can be found in *The Moon through the signs* and *The Moon through the houses* on pages 198–203.

Take it back to your birth chart

On your chart, draw an arrow next to the Moon glyph, and beside it, write the words 'What I need and how I feel.'

Mercury ☿

Living positively: Communicative; intelligent; exchange of ideas

Living negatively: Chattering; superficial; inconsistent

This is the communications planet. Whenever you open your mouth to talk, or when you write something – anything from an SMS to a novel or beyond – or even if you just think or listen to someone, you're using your Mercury. It's the mind planet and it guides how you talk, write, otherwise express yourself and take in information. It's your intellectual process. The sign and house Mercury is in will tell you how you think and express yourself, and even how you negotiate.

Mercury is also the transport planet, and planet of short journeys and commuting. It also governs trade and commerce. Plus it governs your wit, thoughts and thirst for knowledge, and your desire and ability to learn. Do you think quickly? Do you like to analyse things? Are you a fast learner? Can you keep secrets? These sorts of questions will be answered when you learn about your Mercury.

Mercury is the trickster, and it's also the quicksilver planet. If someone is a fast talker or a smooth talker, it's thanks to their Mercury. If they think too hard, or overthink, or can't make decisions, look to their Mercury for an explanation.

Where's your Mercury?

Is your Mercury in a Fire sign (Aries, Leo or Sagittarius), an Earth sign (Taurus, Virgo or Capricorn), a Water sign (Cancer, Scorpio or Pisces) or an Air sign (Gemini, Libra or Aquarius)? Below is a brief overview of what it means to have your Mercury in a particular element:

❖ **Fire sign**: you're likely to shoot from the lip.

❖ **Earth sign**: you're very good at getting your message across in a grounded fashion.

❖ **Air sign**: you're inclined more towards intellectualism.

❖ **Water sign**: you pick up unspoken signals, and assess body language.

Keywords for what Mercury represents: how you talk; the way you connect mentally; your ideas; how you listen; how you exchange ideas. Can also be related to transport, how you learn, how rational you are, and your wit.

Interpretations for Mercury in each sign and house of the birth chart can be found in *Mercury through the signs* and *Mercury through the houses* on pages 205–209.

Take it back to your birth chart

On your chart, draw an arrow next to the Mercury glyph, and beside it, write the words 'How I communicate.'

Venus ♀

Living positively: Loving; gentle; caring

Living negatively: Lazy; manipulative; weak-willed

This planet is all about romance and riches – it's your love planet! Venus guides you when you fancy someone, when you fall in love and when you yearn for someone or something from the bottom of your heart.

So, matters of the heart are dealt with by this beautiful, kind and caring planet. Venus is about pleasure, kindness, caresses – things like lacy underwear and all things sweet. In her highest form, Venus is about perfect and ideal relationships. How you relate to others depends a lot on your Venus. Ditto how you fall in love.

Venus is also about attracting. Your Venus tells you who you love and what you love. Discover a person's Venus sign and house placement and you'll have the key to his or her heart. (Whether you can easily turn that key depends a lot on your own chart and how it matches theirs). Venus is also about aesthetics and our appreciation for the finer things in life, such as the arts and music. It's about beauty and luxury. Wealth and partnership also fall under Venus's remit.

However, do note that someone with, say, their Venus in Aquarius will probably want to be caressed far less than someone with their Venus in Cancer. You'll understand the reasons for this once you learn more about the signs and how they go with the planets – coming up later in the book. Eroticism is also part and parcel of Venus. Knowing your Venus will teach you about what you need in a lover.

Knowing a person's Venus sign and house placement can give you some extraordinarily powerful information about how to seduce them! Devotion, connection, harmony, understanding and longing are also Venus words. Venus is the planet that connects us to the Divine Feminine. Your Venus shows you what you feel about love and relationships.

Where's your Venus?
Below is a brief overview of what it means to have your Venus in a particular element:

❖ **Fire sign**: you fall in love faster.

❖ **Earth sign**: you're usually very loyal and true.

❖ **Air sign**: you can be very romantic but tend to be a tad elusive in love – overthinking it rather than feeling it.

❖ **Water sign**: you are often mushy, and sentimental to a fault!

Keywords for what Venus represents: how you love and who you love; how you attract a partner; your idea of romance; your softer side; how you draw abundance; what feels luxurious to you; how you flirt; how you create harmony; how you express affection; how you're sociable/find pleasure.

Interpretations for Venus in each sign and house of the birth chart can be found in *Venus through the signs* and *Venus through the houses* on pages 209–212.

Take it back to your birth chart

On your chart, draw an arrow next to the Venus glyph, and beside it, write the words 'Who and how I love.'

Mars ♂

Living positively: Determination; courage; action

Living negatively: Rage; brutality; brashness

This is the sex planet. Mars is powered by testosterone – but men and women both have a Mars. Without Mars, nothing much would get done – it is our fuel and our rocket; our determination and drive. Take a look at your Mars.

Mars also governs our sex drive, what turns us on and how we get what we want. Do you demand to have things your way, come at things sideways, make a big deal, get a bit shifty? The sign your Mars is in will give you an insight into the ways you chase your goals. Mars is the planet that's all about pursuit. What are you chasing in life? Your Mars will show you what you're after and also how to get it.

Mars is all about desire and action. Aggressive behaviour, lust, anger and even brutishness are all Mars traits, which will be heightened or lessened depending on Mars's sign and house placement in a chart. Mars is arguably the most masculine planet, and is the zodiacal 'partner' of Venus.

Where's your Mars?

Below is a brief overview of what it means to have your Mars in a particular element:

- ❖ **Fire sign**: this is a major gift because it will give you drive; however, you have to be careful not to burn out from pushing yourself too hard and fast.

- ❖ **Earth sign**: this is wonderful to have because you are endowed with the kind of stamina that can run a marathon or pull an all-nighter at work with no dramas.

- ❖ **Air sign**: this is great, because it's a really healthy balance of Mars Fire-power and Air, which allows that Fire to breathe. Air folk tend to have lots of good energy.

- ❖ **Water sign**: this is a conundrum, because Mars wants to race ahead whereas the Water energy is much more Zen. The Water element can dampen the Mars Fire.

Keywords for what Mars represents: how you go after what you want; how you argue; whether you're a fast or slow person; how determined and driven you are; if you can be brash; your anger levels and sexual energy; how competitive you are; your energy levels in general and your sex drive; how you express anger and your willpower.

Interpretations for Mars in each sign and house of the birth chart can be found in *Mars through the signs* and *Mars through the houses* on pages 212–214.

Take it back to your birth chart

On your chart, draw an arrow next to the Mars glyph, and beside it, write the words 'How I chase and get what I want.'

Jupiter ♃

Living positively: Faith; excitement; adventure, joy

Living negatively: Overindulgence; pompousness; arrogance; risk

This planet is known as the 'greater benefic', which basically means that everything Jupiter touches is blessed. When you look at Jupiter in your chart, you're essentially looking at the good luck charm you were born with. Jupiter is the planet that endows you with the confidence to believe in yourself. It's the amplification planet, sometimes known as the 'lotsa' planet.

Jupiter is also the planet of joy, freedom and adventure, and it can see the big picture. It's also the planet that gives you faith in your Self and the cosmos. Your Jupiter is where you take chances and seize opportunities – this massive planet helps you to grow. Wherever you find Jupiter in a person's chart, is where they like to have fun.

But Jupiter has two sides. On the one hand, a Jupiterian vibe is a jolly, cheery Father Christmas vibe. On the other hand, this is the planet that's all about faith, and seeking life's meaning. Perhaps the meaning of life is to be jolly!

Morals, confidence and luck – or lack thereof – also come under Jupiter's remit. It's no surprise that where we are confident is where we tend to be lucky. Jupiter can also exaggerate wildly, overdo it excessively and tip from confidence into arrogance. Wherever you find Jupiter in someone's chart, is where she or he can get all the glory for being awesome, or come across as an arrogant so-and-so!

Where's your Jupiter?

Below is a brief overview of what it means to have your Jupiter in a particular element:

❖ **Fire sign**: you're likely to have 'lotsa' excitement and drama.

❖ **Earth sign**: you're likely to have 'lotsa' staying power, and practical ideas that can also be quite lucrative.

❖ **Water sign**: you're likely to have 'lotsa' feelings – good feelings, difficult feelings; 'all the feels', as they say.

❖ **Air sign**: you can expect 'lotsa' good ideas, room to move and 'lotsa' social life.

Keywords for what Jupiter represents: whether or not you feel lucky; how lucky you're likely to be; how optimistic you are; where you feel/are blessed; how adventurous you are; your life philosophies and perspective; if you think big or small; your degree of open-mindedness.

Interpretations for Jupiter in each sign and house of the birth chart can be found in *Jupiter through the signs* and *Jupiter through the houses* on pages 215–217.

Take it back to your birth chart

On your chart, draw an arrow next to the Jupiter glyph, and beside it, write the words 'Where I am extra lucky and/or blessed.'

Saturn ♄

Living positively: Commitment; discipline; integrity; longevity

Living negatively: Fear, barriers; depression; hard-heartedness

Saturn has a fearsome reputation as the taskmaster of the zodiac. Saturn is the stench of reality up your nose: the hard facts, and the lessons you didn't want to learn. Wherever you have Saturn in your chart, you must face the music and work hard; it's where you have a lot of lessons coming to you in this lifetime. At least once you know the placement of your Saturn, you'll more or less know where to expect those challenges. And the challenges that you overcome are the lessons than hone you into a more evolved being.

Saturn is about structure, challenges and our fears, as well as being the planet in our chart that governs work and discipline. Saturn is the slowest-moving of the planets that can be seen with the naked eye. Saturn is cold and calculating and wants his pound of flesh. He was once known as the karma planet, and is all about 'you reap what you sow'. Does that phrase make you shiver? It's Saturn all over. Learn a Saturn lesson, change your behaviour, and change your karma!

That's just one side of Saturn, though. Saturn's feminine side is the wise old crone. She may no longer be a beauty but she doesn't care: she's beyond all that. She will dispense what she knows to you. Wherever your Saturn is, you can accumulate wisdom. For example, someone with Saturn in the 9th house may gain wisdom through study or travel.

However, Saturn brings fear, including a fear of not having enough. Saturn is all about wisdom, and facing the truth, and having integrity, and doing what you said you would. Where you find Saturn in your chart, though, you'll also find a big ball of your fears. Saturn can be repressive: he doesn't shy from giving bad news you were trying to ignore, and wherever he is in your chart, he sets limits. These can be useful on some occasions, and a drag on others. Saturn doesn't care if he's being a drag.

Where's your Saturn?
Below is a brief overview of what it means to have your Saturn in a particular element:

❖ **Fire sign**: this can be frustrating – it may mean you're forced to slow down by life when you want to race ahead.

❖ **Earth sign**: this is arguably the easiest to handle, as Earth signs don't assume too much and Saturn won't let anyone assume too much!

❖ **Air sign**: this is wonderful for making long-lasting decisions and formulating ideas. It's important to let your ideas flow.

❖ **Water sign**: can be tricky because the Water signs want to let their feelings flow and Saturn is all about limits and restrictions.

Keywords for what Saturn represents: your lessons this lifetime; what you fear; what makes you sad; what can depress or limit you; where the brakes are on; where you can really commit and go the long haul; where you're rock solid. Also, your patience levels; your self-discipline; how conventional you are; your ambition, and how responsible you are.

Interpretations for Saturn in each sign and house of the birth chart can be found in *Saturn through the signs* and *Saturn through the houses* on pages 217–220.

Take it back to your birth chart

On your chart, draw an arrow next to the Saturn glyph, and beside it, write the words 'Where I have a lot to learn/what scares me.'

Uranus ♅

Living positively: Progress; change; unexpected surprises; breakthroughs; non-conformity

Living negatively: Chaos; wrecking; unreliability; rushing

This is the innovative maverick of the zodiac. Wherever you have Uranus in your chart, you want to break free; it's where you're going to do things your way, where you don't really care too much what anyone thinks, and where you can function autonomously. Freedom is a keyword for Uranus. This is one planet that absolutely doesn't want to be fenced in. Wherever you have Uranus in your chart, you're striving for independence. Uranus is also the planet of bolts from the blue and sudden reversals.

If someone has Uranus very prominent in their chart – for example if it's right on their ascendant or in the same place as their Sun – chances are they are surprising and different, probably in a really good way. Uranus is all about liberation. It destroys traditions and breaks down authority. As a result, Uranus is the planet of modernity – it drags us kicking and screaming and shocked out of the past and into our future. Unsurprisingly, Uranus is also associated with anarchy and unpredictability.

Uranus rules chaos, and wherever the planet is in your chart, you're quite possibly inclined to being something of a loose cannon.

Where's your Uranus?
Astrologers don't tend to talk about Uranus through the elements so much as Uranus through the various signs over generations. People with Uranus in Virgo, for example, were all born from 1961 to 1969, after which Uranus moved into Libra, where it stayed until 1975.

Uranus will define where there was massive change. The Uranus in Virgo generation, for example, brought hippies, flower power and the rise and rise of alternative health therapies and practices, while the Uranus in Libra generation saw the advent of 'free love' and even more challenges to conventional relationships.

As this stage of your astrological journey, it's more useful to think about which house your Uranus is in. Later we'll look at the connections Uranus is making to your other planets. Wherever you find Uranus in your chart (which house), you have the chance for radical change and excitement.

Keywords for what Uranus represents: where you want to be free; where you're liberated or want to be liberated; where you're evolving and how you evolve; where you're original, inventive, unpredictable, rash and untamable; where you cut the ties that bind to break away.

Interpretations for Uranus in each sign and house of the birth chart can be found in *Uranus through the signs* and *Uranus through the houses* on pages 221–223.

can be found in *Uranus through the signs* and *Uranus through the houses* on pages 221–223.

Take it back to your birth chart

On your chart, draw an arrow next to the Uranus glyph, and beside it, write the words 'Where I can't be controlled!'

Neptune ♆

Living positively: Enlightenment; inspiration; dreams; connection; mysticism; sacrifice

Living negatively: No boundaries; substance abuse; delusions; disappointment

Neptune is the inspirational planet of dreams and soulmates. In whichever house you find Neptune in your chart is the area where you romanticize life. Neptune is about the Divine. It's also about drugs and alcohol. But how do these go together? Understand this and you'll understand Neptune and astrology a little better: life is about extremes, so with Neptune, altered states are part of the remit. At one end of the altered-state 'OMG I've just seen God!' spectrum is the person tripping on drugs, and at the other end, is the person who's connected to the Divine through more regular methods.

Similarly, Neptune is about deception at one end of the spectrum and about fantasy, and even about movies, at the other – Hollywood is all smoke and mirrors, after all.

The house in which you find Neptune in your chart can be where you're a visionary or a poet or an artist, or even a martyr. But it can also be where you dissolve completely, like a droplet of water into an ocean. It's about meditation and enlightenment at one end of the spectrum and about addiction and intoxicants at the other. Idealization, trances, spirit and the paranormal are also Neptunian.

Where's your Neptune?
As Neptune is another slow-moving generational planet, we tend not to talk about it in terms of which element it's in, but rather which sign it's in, and also which house it's in on a chart. For example, those born with Neptune in Capricorn – from January 1984 to August 1998 – are the benevolent entrepreneurs, Neptune being the planet of benevolence and Capricorn the sign of business.

Conversely, the Neptune in Aquarius generation – January 1998 to August 2011 – is often called the universal free spirits, Neptune being about the mystical and Aquarius being the universal sign. This is something you can delve into further as you continue your studies. For now, what's important is to look at the house Neptune occupies in your chart. Wherever you find Neptune (which house), you'll have the potential for inspiration. Later, we'll look at how Neptune is connected to the other planets in your chart.

Keywords for what Neptune represents: your connection to the Divine and spirit; what inspires you, and how you inspire others; where you are often lost and confused; your relationship with music, drugs and alcohol; your psychic ability.

Interpretations for Neptune in each sign and house of the birth chart can be found in *Neptune through the signs* and *Neptune through the houses* on pages 224–226.

Take it back to your birth chart

On your chart, draw an arrow next to the Neptune glyph on your chart, and beside it, write the words 'Where I dream, inspired and can be inspired/can be confused.'

Pluto ♀ ♇

Living positively: Transformation; healing crisis; passion; power

Living negatively: Destruction; power struggles; violence

Pluto is the Lord of the Underworld and not a planet to be trifled with. On the upside, Pluto is also a fantastic magician and is responsible for any transformation we effect in our lives. Pluto represents the birth, death and rebirth cycle. It's the planet that detoxes – the great plumber of the zodiac. Got an issue? Trust Pluto to flush out the toxins.

Pluto is where we can go into the abyss. Pluto can transform by annihilation! Pluto is also an obsessive power-monger. You might think all this sounds very dark and cruel and brutal, and there's no doubt that controlling and manipulative Pluto can be all of those things. But Pluto in your chart also shows where you can change your world.

Pluto is subtle and sometimes even intangible, but its power can slam you up against the wall like a character that's been hexed in a *Harry Potter* film. Pluto finishes what needs to be let go, and empowers us. Think of Pluto as the de-clutterer of the zodiac – it gets rid of all the rubbish. Plutonic upheavals can often be seen, in retrospect, as a 'healing crisis'.

Where's your Pluto?
Pluto is the slowest moving of all the planets, so once again we think less about which element it's in, than which sign. Look at where in your chart it is (which house). That is where you have the chance for rebirth, and also for obsession. Later in the book, we'll look at how Pluto connects with the other planets in your chart.

Keywords for what Pluto represents: where you're in control, or you want to be; where you're obsessive; where you erupt, engage in power struggles, try to dominate or are dominated; your depths; the side of you that you keep hidden; your shadow – your dark side; your destructive side; where you are reborn; how manipulative you are.

Interpretations for Pluto in each sign and house of the birth chart can be found in *Pluto through the signs* and *Pluto through the houses* on pages 227–229.

Take it back to your birth chart

On your chart, draw an arrow next to the Pluto glyph, and beside it, write the words 'Where I control, break down, am reborn.'

The positive and negative sides of the planets

It's fair to say that, like most people, each of the planets has positive and negative sides. The Sun, Moon and Mercury change like the wind in terms of whether they're regarded as positive or negative; it depends on how they are placed in a chart.

Venus and Jupiter are traditionally regarded as benefics, or easier planets, while Mars and Saturn are traditionally regarded as malefics, or more challenging planets. Mars can indeed be brash and Saturn can be a drag, but I hold the more modern belief that they are both definitely useful. Mars, for example, gives us determination and drive – where would we be without that? Meanwhile Saturn makes us commit, and brings order.

Astrologers seem to be divided over whether or not Uranus and Neptune are easy or difficult. I see them more as exciting and mystical, respectively. Pluto is powerful and will make us crumble when we need to – but this process can be a good thing, even if it doesn't feel like it at the time.

Whether the positive or negative side comes out depends on how the planets in the chart are connected to each other, and also on what's going on in the skies right now that may be impacting the planets in a birth chart. So while your chart shows where the planets were at the moment you were born, as you know, the planets didn't stop moving after that wonderful event! No, they have kept on moving ever since; so what astrologers do is look at where the planets are now, compared to where they were when you were born. And depending on how far apart the still-moving (aka 'transiting') planets are from where they were when you were born, we make deductions and predictions.

As you can see, each planet features both ends of the negative–positive spectrum. That's astrology. As you learn more, you'll start to understand how to manifest the good side and lessen the darker sign of each planet's energy. Some of it you are born with and some of it can be put into play just by your desire to bring out the best in your chart.

Planetary keywords

Finally, here's a brief round-up of the main characteristics of the planets to help you remember them. In your mind, reduce these descriptions down to keywords and the ideas that spring to mind when you're thinking about the planets.

❖ **Your Sun**, if you're living positively, is where you shine, where you're generous or magnanimous. If you're living negatively, it can be where you show off or have ego issues.

❖ **Your Moon** is where you feel deeply, and look after others. Or where you're downright needy, timid or even emotionally repressed.

❖ **Your Mercury** can be where you talk and listen and generally express yourself. Or where you're a gossip or a fibber, or where you skim through things you should take more time over.

❖ **Your Venus** is where you love and relate to other people, or where you're vain or lazy.

❖ **Your Mars** is where you go for it and chase your dreams, are courageous and energized. Or it can be where you're brash, argumentative and/or destructive.

❖ **Your Jupiter** is where you're lucky, cheerful, likeable and full of faith. Or it can be where you're over-confident, complacent, overbearing and/or plain foolish.

❖ **Your Saturn** can be where you're hard-working, sensible, self-controlled and strategic, or where you're rigid with fear, narrow-minded, hesitant or stuck.

❖ **Your Uranus** can be where you dare to be different; where you don't care what anyone else says; where you do things your way and break down the barriers. Or it can be where you're a perverse loose cannon.

❖ **Your Neptune** is where you're inspiring and inspired: where you connect with the Divine and you uplift. But it's also where you can be deceptive, confused, over-idealistic and needlessly worried.

❖ **Your Pluto** is where you can transform anything from the inside out; it's where you have power and magic, and can rid yourself of dead wood. Or it's where you can be a power-hungry control-monger.

SUMMARY

In this chapter, you've learned the basic astrological characteristic of the 10 planets – understanding these is intrinsic to astrology because we all have *all* of the planets in our chart. Even knowing which element or sign your planets are in will be revelatory. As you learn more and discover the houses your planets are in, and the connections they're making to other planets in your chart - coming up soon - you'll glean even more fascinating information about yourself and others.

Chapter 5
Exploring the zodiac signs

So far, you've worked with your chart to locate all 12 zodiac signs, to work out which planets are in which signs, and to identify the sign that rules each house; you've also learned that each sign is a unique combination and expression of its element, quality and polarity. Now let's delve a little deeper into the signs and discover what they can reveal about you.

You'll know from your birth dates that you 'are' one of the 12 zodiac signs, which are also known as Sun signs. For example, you may be an Aries Sun sign or a Pisces Sun sign and so on (before you started studying astrology, you may have called your Sun sign your Star sign). By now though, you'll be aware that you have planets other than your Sun in your chart, and many of them will be in other signs.

Your Moon sign, Mercury sign, Pluto sign, and so on are as important as your Sun sign, and they move towards giving you a complete picture of yourself. For this reason, it's important to get to know the traits of *all 12 signs*, which is what you're going to do now.

As you learned in Chapter 3, each sign is oh-so different from its neighbour. In fact, if anything, the signs that have the most in common are the opposite signs. This corresponds with the idea that opposites can either attract or repel, often quite dramatically.

The signs' ruling planets

At this point, it's good for you to know that each zodiac sign is said to have a 'ruling planet' that governs it and flavours it with certain personality traits. Below, you'll find the ruling planet for each sign (each planet rules two signs, and the luminaries – the Sun and Moon – rule one each).

- ❖ **Aries** is ruled by **Mars**
- ❖ **Taurus** is ruled by **Venus**
- ❖ **Gemini** is ruled by **Mercury**
- ❖ **Cancer** is ruled by the **Moon**
- ❖ **Leo** is ruled by the **Sun**
- ❖ **Virgo** is ruled by **Mercury**
- ❖ **Libra** is ruled by **Venus**
- ❖ **Scorpio** is ruled by **Mars** in traditional astrology, and **Pluto** in modern astrology
- ❖ **Sagittarius** is ruled by **Jupiter**
- ❖ **Capricorn** is ruled by **Saturn**
- ❖ **Aquarius** is ruled by **Saturn** in traditional astrology and by **Uranus** in modern astrology
- ❖ **Pisces** is ruled by **Jupiter** in traditional astrology and by **Neptune** in modern astrology

Take it back to your birth chart

Make a note of your ruling planet.

Your ruling planet is the planet that rules your Rising Sign.

For example:

My Rising Sign is Gemini, therefore Mercury is my ruling planet

Your turn...

My Rising Sign is _____, therefore _____ is my ruling planet

The meaning of the signs

In Chapter 3, you learned that the four elements (Fire, Earth, Air and Water), three qualities (Cardinal, Fixed and Mutable) and two polarities (yang/yin) are the basic, underlying nature of each zodiac sign. Let's now go into more depth on the key characteristics of each sign.

The following descriptions do not specifically or exclusively apply to people with the Sun in that sign. They can apply to you as a Leo or a Virgo, or whatever Sun sign you are, but remember, they also apply to the other planets and points in your chart (including houses and angles – you'll learn about these later), so try to memorize the main idea of each sign. As you read on, reduce the sign descriptions to keywords in your head.

In the *Take it back to your birth chart* exercises at the end of each sign section, I've asked you to pull together some of the information you've learned so far to see if you can find a correlation between what you find in your chart, and you as a person.

Here are some simple examples of how those 'interpretations' could look:

❖ Mars in Capricorn in your 10th house could make you very ambitious (Capricorn) and proactive (Mars) in your career (10th house).

❖ Mercury in Virgo in your 4th house would mean you're often thinking (Mercury) about what you can do to help (Virgo) at home (4th house).

❖ Venus in Gemini in the 1st house could make you come across as (1st house) someone who loves (Venus) to chat (Gemini).

Aries ♈

❖ Element: Fire

❖ Quality: Cardinal

❖ Ruling planet: Mars

❖ Opposite sign: Libra

❖ Keywords: I am

❖ Harmonizes most easily with: Aries, Gemini, Leo, Libra, Sagittarius and Aquarius

Aries is the first sign of the zodiac, and Aries people and the sign are 'out there' – forward-moving, burning bright, wanting to set the world on fire. Aries is ruled by the fiery planet Mars – the firepower in the engine of the zodiac.

Wallflowers and timid people need not apply to this sign, basically.

Aries races past anyone or anything that stands still or isn't paying attention. Wherever you have Aries in your chart, you're in a hurry. It's where you're determined and driven: where you can get things done. Make sure you're not being 'crude' in your rush to get things done, though. Aries people have a fire burning in them (which Water and Earth people sometimes want to put out!). There's often a twinkle in their eye about it, though, which is a good thing. However, it's important not to let the Aries energy wear you down or burn you out. It's a high consumer of energy and very yang. The softer yin elements in the chart need to be given attention too.

Take it back to your birth chart

Which house does Aries rule? Which planet(s), if any, do you have in Aries?

Can you see a correlation between what you find in your chart and you as a person? Take a look at the examples above and then come up with your own interpretations.

Taurus ♉

❖ Element: Earth

❖ Quality: Fixed

❖ Ruling planet: Venus

- ❖ Keywords: I have

- ❖ Opposite sign: Scorpio

- ❖ Harmonizes most easily with: Taurus, Cancer, Virgo, Scorpio, Capricorn and Pisces

Taurus, represented by the Bull, is a slow and contented creature, at least most of the time. Taurus can see red like an angry bull, yes, but living harmoniously, Taurus is the slower and more content Bull chewing the cud in the field. Wherever Taurus is in your chart, you'll find your sensual but also your stubborn side. Taurus also has a really indulgent side and is often concerned with money. The thing you need to know about Taureans is that what they really want is to feel as comfortable as they possibly can – pretty much everything they do in life has that aim and purpose.

Think of the Bull rolled over on its side in the paddock on a hot, sunny day: that's where Taurus wants to be. Wherever you have Taurus in your chart, there's a touch of the magical Taurean ability to endure, possibly to attract cash, possibly to unleash your sensual side.

Being an Earth sign, Taurus is also practical. It knows how to earn what's needed to pay for the desired indulgences, because it's ruled by the elegant and feminine, pleasure-seeking planet Venus. My favourite observation is that if someone ever asks to lick whipped cream off your stomach, they probably have Taurus strong in their chart! In other words, they could be Taurean or have a Taurus Moon or Taurus Rising, or just lots of planets in Taurus.

Take it back to your birth chart

Which house does Taurus rule? Which planet(s), if any, do you have in Taurus?

Can you see a correlation between what you find in your chart and you as a person? Take a look at the examples above and then come up with your own interpretations.

Gemini ♊

❖ Element: Air

❖ Quality: Mutable

❖ Ruling planet: Mercury

❖ Keywords: I think

❖ Opposite sign: Sagittarius

❖ Harmonizes most easily with: Aries, Gemini, Leo, Libra, Sagittarius and Aquarius

Geminis are the flirts of the zodiac. They are thinkers and talkers – chatty to the point of talking the hind legs off a donkey when they're really on a roll! Perhaps unsurprisingly, given their inquiring minds, this sign is also one of the most intellectual of the zodiac. Gemini is all about being smart and grasping concepts as readily as people have toast for breakfast. Gemini energy is also the rapier wit. Wherever you have Gemini in your chart (via a planet, cusp or angle), there's a sort of intellectual freedom of movement. The wonderful thing about the Gemini energy is that it's inquisitiveness incarnate.

Wherever you have Gemini in your chart, there's a playfulness, and a willingness to learn and to connect mentally. Sometimes a lot of Gemini energy can mean too much head energy, and arguably not enough heart energy, but you can counter that by really connecting with your Venus. Once you've learned more about astrology, you'll know how to do that – but in a nutshell, it's about doing Venusian things such as embracing your femininity or all things feminine.

Also, wherever you have Gemini in your chart, you can always talk things through – it's where you're open to communication. Gemini has a 'tread lightly' feel. As for the infamous rumours about Gemini being two-faced, I'd be far more inclined to think of Gemini as quick to explore the options. Or, okay, maybe a teensy bit silver-tongued occasionally, but in the very nicest possible way – at least most of the time. Gemini is sometimes garrulous. Often vociferous. Awesome.

Take it back to your birth chart

Which house does Gemini rule? Which planet(s), if any, do you have in Gemini?

Can you see a correlation between what you find in your chart and you as a person? Take a look at the examples above and then come up with your own interpretations.

Cancer ♋

❖ Element: Water

❖ Quality: Cardinal

❖ Ruling planet: the Moon

❖ Keywords: I feel

❖ Opposite sign: Capricorn

❖ Harmonizes most easily with: Taurus, Cancer, Virgo, Scorpio, Capricorn and Pisces

For me, the easiest way to understand the sign of Cancer is to think of its symbol, the Crab – which has a very hard shell and a super-soft and vulnerable underbelly. It goes at things sideways and it clings on. Cancer is a slightly awkward mixture of a super-soft and easily sentimental Water sign and a dynamic, self-starting Cardinal sign. Sometimes those two traits clash. And sometimes they create formidable, functional people. Wherever you have Cancer in your chart, you're extra-sensitive. More than anything, Cancer is a very feminine sign, arguably the sign of the Goddess.

My wonderful late, great teacher, Jonathan Cainer, once remarked that it's ironic that the most sensitive sign has the most disturbing name. Remember, we incarnate into the charts we do because we have lessons to learn. Wherever you have the sign of Cancer in your chart – by planet, cusp or angle – you're learning to be sensitive without being over-sensitive. Cancer is a very female energy, and like many women, it's very emotional and even sentimental. However, we all know that women are more than just that! Women and Cancerian energy are both also very strong. Cancer also rules memory and history.

Take it back to your birth chart

Which house does Cancer rule? Which planet(s), if any, do you have in Cancer?

Can you see a correlation between what you find in your chart and you as a person? Take a look at the examples above and then come up with your own interpretations.

Leo ♌

❖ Element: Fire

❖ Quality: Fixed

❖ Ruling planet: the Sun

❖ Keywords: I will

❖ Opposite sign: Aquarius

❖ Harmonizes most easily with: Aries, Gemini, Leo, Libra, Sagittarius and Aquarius

Leos, oh Leos, how we adore you, right? I have to say that: Leo wants to shine and it does so; it wants to be adored and it is. Leo is generous and magnanimous, but it can also lord it over us mere minions, casting shadows under the brightness of its guiding planet, the Sun. Wherever you have Leo in your chart, you can stand out. Vitality is a powerful word to associate with this sign. Think 'Sun burns bright'.

Leo is a pretty amazing sign, characterized by ambition, creativity and dignity. Leos like to be the centre of attention and they often are. But once again, we all have Leo in our chart, by planet, sign or house cusp, and there's a part of us that can access this hot energy. Remember, ruled by the Sun, the Leo energy thinks (or knows!) that everything revolves around it. Leo energy needs praising – it needs to feel as though it's the king or queen, and it most certainly doesn't like to be displaced. It's also a very proud energy. Even though Leo can err like the rest of us, Leos do not like to have their mistakes rubbed in their face. Leo is also the drama king or queen of the zodiac. Leo turns heads.

Take it back to your birth chart

Which house does Leo rule? Which planet(s), if any, do you have in Leo?

Can you see a correlation between what you find in your chart and you as a person? Take a look at the examples above and then come up with your own interpretations.

Virgo ♍

+ Element: Earth

+ Quality: Mutable

+ Ruling planet: Mercury

+ Keywords: I analyse

+ Opposite sign: Pisces

+ Harmonizes most easily with: Taurus, Cancer, Virgo, Scorpio, Capricorn and Pisces

Virgo is a classically down-to-earth Earth sign, and Virgos are awesome people to have around. They are practical, helpful and reasonable – sometimes almost too much so: they're the ones who notice and remind you that your car tyres are going bald or that there's a bit of dust gathering behind your TV. Where you have Virgo in your chart, you're good at analysing and sorting things out.

Virgo is sensible and serious in one way but creative in another, and that can be an awesome combination. When looking to hire assistants, I've been known to advertise specifically for Virgos because Virgo takes care of the details and takes responsibility. Virgo is methodical and precise and errs on the healthy side, most of the time.

Virgo energy can sometimes be rather earnest, but that's because Virgo is guided by the communications planet and wants to get a message across properly, even if that sometimes means being nit-picky. Before you get all sanctimonious with your Virgo friends, though, remember we all have Virgo somewhere in our chart, be it with planets, house cusps or angles. Virgo gets a less than stellar rap as it's not as in your face as some signs. However, it's strongly associated with the Goddess – we all know women who are happy to work tirelessly and even thanklessly in the background, and that's very Virgo.

Take it back to your birth chart

Which house does Virgo rule? Which planet(s), if any, do you have in Virgo?

Can you see a correlation between what you find in your chart and you as a person? Take a look at the examples above and then come up with your own interpretations.

Libra ♎

- ❖ Element: Air
- ❖ Quality: Cardinal
- ❖ Ruling planet: Venus
- ❖ Keywords: I balance
- ❖ Opposite sign: Aries
- ❖ Harmonizes most easily with: Aries, Gemini, Leo, Libra, Sagittarius and Aquarius

This is the sign guided by Venus, the planet of love and abundance. It's often noted that Libra is the only sign that isn't represented by a living being, and that as an Air sign, these people are all in their heads. As if being a set of scales and not a Lion or a Virgin or a Twin something is not a good thing... But wait up. Libra is ruled by Venus, which is also the planet of the Divine Mother and the Divine Feminine and Divine Love. How much love and feelings do you think you can fit into one sign?

Libra loves love and loves relationships and flirting; it craves one on one and beauty and harmony. Wherever you have Libra in your chart, you're all about getting things right, and justice, and making things as smooth as possible. Libra has a reputation for being indecisive, but I believe that's just really lazy astrology. Libra is the balance, the scales, and so of course it weighs up all sides of an equation before making a decision. Libra energy is go-between energy. It always wants the truth, preferably presented in as pleasant a fashion possible.

Which house does Libra rule? Which planet(s), if any, do you have in Libra?

Can you see a correlation between what you find in your chart and you as a person? Take a look at the examples above and then come up with your own interpretations.

Scorpio ♏

✦ Element: Water

✦ Quality: Fixed

✦ Ruling planet: Mars (in traditional astrology) and Pluto (in modern astrology)

✦ Keywords: I lust

✦ Opposite sign: Taurus

✦ Harmonizes most easily with: Taurus, Cancer, Virgo, Scorpio. Capricorn and Pisces

Scorpio is represented by an animal that can sting you to death. Everyone has a bit of Scorpio in them, have you noticed? Scorpios apologize to me for 'being Scorpio' quite often! But we all have Scorpio in our chart. Take a look now and find the Scorpio symbol in your chart – it will rule at least one house and potentially one or more planets. That's where you'll find your shadow side. Scorpio is the energy that helps us to understand life's mysteries. It faces the things others shy away from, and sometimes it forces us to face them too.

Scorpio is the Dark Side but there's a good side to that, and we shouldn't fear it, because it's powerful. Think of the Dark Mother or the crone: they know things. Scorpio knows things and we can learn its lessons if we aren't closed off with fear. Wherever you have Scorpio in your chart, there's a layer of Scorpionic traits. It's true the Scorpio holds grudges that can last a lifetime, and that's a real pity, if you ask me. But it's part of the Great Human Fabric, right? I'll say it again: we all have Scorpio somewhere in our chart! Plus, Scorpio is sexy.

Take it back to your birth chart

Which house does Scorpio rule? Which planet(s), if any, do you have in Scorpio?

Can you see a correlation between what you find in your chart and you as a person? Take a look at the examples above and then come up with your own interpretations.

Sagittarius ♐

♦ Element: Fire

♦ Quality: Mutable

♦ Ruling planet: Jupiter

♦ Keywords: I see

♦ Opposite sign: Gemini

♦ Harmonizes most easily with: Aries, Gemini, Leo, Libra, Sagittarius and Aquarius

Sagittarius is pretty much the luckiest sign of the zodiac, and the good news is, we all have Sagittarius somewhere in our charts – that's where things flow. (We also look to the planet Jupiter for this, but Sagittarius carries a lot of Jupiterian energy and vice versa.) But we shouldn't confuse Sagittarian cheerfulness with superficiality. In fact, Sagittarius has a huge capacity for big thoughts and seeing the big picture of life. It can be preachy sometimes, but that's because Sagittarius energy wants to explore and adventure and broaden life's perspectives, especially by studying and teaching.

With Sagittarius, the danger is complacency, whatever that looks like for you. Carelessness is also a potential issue wherever you have Sagittarius in your chart. Sagittarius has a devil-may-care thing going on and it's not afraid to show it. Of course, many great achievements come via taking great risks and Sagittarius is not risk averse. So go easy and don't bet the farm if you have lots of Sagittarius planets – well, unless you don't mind the possibility of losing the farm!

Take it back to your birth chart

Which house does Sagittarius rule? Which planet(s), if any, do you have in Sagittarius?

Can you see a correlation between what you find in your chart and you as a person? Take a look at the examples above and then come up with your own interpretations.

Capricorn ♑

❖   Element: Earth

❖   Quality: Cardinal

❖   Ruling planet: Saturn

❖   Keywords: I use

❖   Opposite sign: Cancer

❖   Harmonizes most easily with: Taurus, Cancer, Virgo, Scorpio, Capricorn and Pisces

Capricorn is a very intense energy that can really bowl you over. These guys are guided by the steamroller planet of the zodiac, aka Saturn, which is one of the reasons why people with lots of planets in Capricorn are often very successful: they steamroller their way through things – not in a bad way but in a serious way that can sometimes just crush their opposition. Capricorn is the energy which understands that 'Rome wasn't built in a day' on various levels. For one thing, Capricorn understands that quality sometimes takes time; for another, it's the traditional sign and it has a sense of why we are where we are.

Capricorn energy is disciplined and needs order, and it isn't afraid to ask for it. It's the energy of hard facts and figures, and it has little or no room for woo-woo (for that, see where you have Pisces in your chart). Capricorn is clear and precise and it can evaluate things in wonderful ways; you have access to that energy wherever you have planets in Capricorn and/or houses ruled by Capricorn. This sign can be stern, and it also corresponds to the government.

Take it back to your birth chart

Which house does Capricorn rule? Which planet(s), if any, do you have in Capricorn?

Can you see a correlation between what you find in your chart and you as a person? Take a look at the examples above and then come up with your own interpretations.

Aquarius ♒

❖ Element: Air

❖ Quality: Fixed

❖ Ruling planet: Saturn (in traditional astrology) and Uranus (in modern astrology)

❖ Keywords: I know

❖ Opposite sign: Leo

❖ Harmonizes most easily with: Aries, Gemini, Leo, Libra, Sagittarius and Aquarius

This is another sign that lives in its head a lot. Some people assume that as a Water Bearer, Aquarius is a Water sign, but it is Air and Air and Air. Aquarians are lofty thinkers – pragmatic and unusual. Eric Francis, one of my fellow astrologers, calls them 'Aqueerius' and the name could hardly be more apt! The 'crazy ones, the misfits, the rebels, the troublemakers, the round pegs in the square holes... the ones who see things differently' that Steve Jobs spoke of almost certainly had/have a lot of Aquarian energy in their charts, and as a matter of fact, Aquarius's modern ruling planet, Uranus, also rules technology, the internet and computers.

Wherever you have Aquarius in your chart (for example, a planet in Aquarius or the house with Aquarius on the cusp), you don't care so much about what other people think of you – not deep down, anyway. The more 'Aqueerius' you are, the more you need to embrace your eccentricities. Aquarius also has a strong maverick vibe; it can set us free because it refuses to be controlled or obedient.

That's not to say that Aquarians can't be well-behaved – they can, but only when it suits them. They do have Saturn as their traditional ruling planet, which gives them a certain gravity. Aquarians are the inventors, the forward-thinking individuals, and they are sometimes too honest and often charmingly unusual.

Take it back to your birth chart

Which house does Aquarius rule? Which planet(s), if any, do you have in Aquarius?

Can you see a correlation between what you find in your chart and you as a person? Take a look at the examples above and then come up with your own interpretations.

Pisces)(

- ❖ Element: Water
- ❖ Quality: Mutable
- ❖ Ruling planet: Jupiter (in traditional astrology) and Neptune (in modern astrology)
- ❖ Keywords: I believe
- ❖ Opposite sign: Virgo
- ❖ Harmonizes most easily with: Taurus, Cancer, Virgo, Scorpio. Capricorn and Pisces

This is the sign of escape and dreams. If you want to know about Pisces, think about two fishes swimming in very deep water; and now, in your imagination, try to capture them both. It's hard to do and the same can be said for Pisces energy. Just when you think you have a handle on it, it slips away. People with a lot of Pisces in their chart (by house, angle or planet) are will-o'-the-wisps. Somehow they live in the world of dreams, and sometimes they are so dreamy themselves, they inspire you and end up in the world of your dreams.

They can be very seductive or very confusing. They often seem rather ungrounded, or perhaps they just come across as wonderfully mystical. They are yin – unless they are pushing themselves too hard or upset, in which case they can become very yang.

Pisces loves art, film and literature – anything they can immerse themselves in (immerse, a Water sign, get it?) and drown their sorrows and follow their soul's passion. Many of them talk about the soul a lot, or about being 'soulful'. Wherever you have Pisces in your chart, there's this elusive, slightly difficult to put your finger on, dream-like quality. You may not be surprised to hear that in modern astrology, Pisces is actually ruled by the mystical, misty blue planet Neptune. Pisces is psychic.

Take it back to your birth chart

Which house does Pisces rule? Which planet(s), if any, do you have in Pisces?

Can you see a correlation between what you find in your chart and you as a person? Take a look at the examples above and then come up with your own interpretations.

SUMMARY

In this chapter, you've built on your basic understanding of the signs of the zodiac. The quicker you get to know the signs, the better. Some astrologers say that the signs are the 'clothes' that the planets and houses put on. For example, if you have Venus in Aries, Venus will exude an Aries feel in the way you love. The more you understand the signs, the more you'll understand how they shape, colour, or even 'perfume' the planets and houses and other points in your chart.

Chapter 6
The angles

Now we come to another of the essential building blocks of astrology. Every birth chart is divided by four angles – when you look at yours you'll see them, shown as lines at approximately 3, 6, 9 and 12 o'clock. The line that runs from around 9 o'clock to 3 o'clock has ASC written on its left end, while the line that runs from around 12 o'clock to 6 o'clock (or thereabouts) has MC written at its top end.

* **The ASC** line is an axis that divides the top and bottom halves of your chart. It has the ASC – the ascendant, or Rising Sign – at one end, and the DES – the descendant – at the other.

* **The MC** line is an axis that divides the left and right hemispheres of your chart. It has the MC – the *Medium Coeli* or Midheaven – at one end and the IC – the *Imum Coeli* – at the other.

The four angles are important because they rule our self, our relationships, our inner lives and our career.

Take it back to your birth chart

Locate the angles on your chart.

❖   The ascendant (or Rising Sign) is marked by its abbreviation (ASC).

❖   The descendant is at the other end of the ASC; it's marked by its abbreviation (DES)

❖   The *Medium Coeli* (or Midheaven) is marked by its abbreviation (MC).

❖   The *Imum Coeli* is at the other end of the MC; it's marked by its abbreviation (IC)

Now let's look at each of the four angles in more detail.

The ascendant (Rising Sign)

Hopefully, you've already identified your ascendant (aka your Rising Sign). So what's it all about? The easiest way to describe your ascendant, which is interchangeably called the Rising Sign, is as the way you come across to people: it's what they register when they meet you for the first time.

The ascendant is sometimes referred to as 'the mask' we wear, which sounds really sinister, but think about it – we do all have a sort of social mask we put on, especially when meeting people for the first time, be it at a party, a work event, or in an interview.

In other words, your Sun sign is your 'real' self, whereas your Rising Sign is the 'face' you put on or the 'mask' you wear. We all do it. So the zodiac sign your Rising Sign is in, is a big thing because you come across very much as that sign. So if you're Scorpio Rising, you come across as Scorpionic – in other words, rather mysterious. And if you're Libra Rising, you exude Libran energy so you're rather charming.

The Rising Sign is also the most personal point on your chart because it's dictated by the exact time and place and date you were born. So someone born at the same moment in time as you were, but on the other side of the world (or even just a few miles away) will have a totally different Rising Sign to you.

In order to understand how the various Rising Signs present, we need to combine the idea of 'the way someone comes across' with the qualities of their Rising Sign. So in very broad terms, we get something like the following descriptions:

Signs on the ascendant

Remember, your Rising Sign is the sign on your 1st house – the sign at 9 o'clock on your chart.

Aries Rising: someone who might be likely to barge in. Fiery, and highly spontaneous. Lit up. Enthusiastic.

Taurus Rising: a person who may be quite stubborn. May be heavy-set. Can be lazy. Someone who comes across as natural and often quite content – except when they're a raging bull!

Gemini Rising: a very talkative person who may appear superficial at times but who really just knows how to keep the conversational wheels greased.

Cancer Rising: someone who serves you food. If female, may have a rather abundant chest. Is warm and homely but can also be quite cutting and bossy.

Leo Rising: may have big hair. Someone who turns heads and can razzle-dazzle. May be rather proud; often the centre of attention.

Virgo Rising: someone with a chaste or modest exterior (which may hide a much wilder side!) A bean counter or a critic; someone who notices the details, and is helpful.

Libra Rising: a person who comes across as harmonious or peaceful. A good negotiator. May be diplomatic. May also be a flatterer who says what others want to hear.

Scorpio Rising: comes across as a mystery. Likes to keep secrets. Has a dark side and knows it. Finds it hard to let people in. Comes across as deep and meaningful.

Sagittarius Rising: the joker in the pack. The person with a permanent grin. Adventurous. May talk a lot of hot air. The student or the law-keeper. A party person.

Capricorn Rising: the serious one – or at least has a serious side. May complain rather a lot. Is quite easily taken seriously. Seems earnest. A good business face.

Aquarius Rising: the person with the bright blue hair – or at least something else about them that seems highly unusual. Crazy eyes! The mad scientist. The wild one. Fun.

Pisces Rising: the dreamer. The person who recites poetry to you. Someone who has their head in the clouds, or appears to. Someone who's in touch with the mystical side of life.

The Rising Sign is how people perceive us. It's our personal style. For example, a Capricorn Sun person would be ambitious and reserved, but coupled with a Sagittarius Rising, he or she would be quite carefree, while also working hard to reach his or her Capricorn goals.

Take it back to your birth chart

Look again at the sign on your ascendant.

My Rising Sign (my ascendant) is in _____, therefore when I walk into a room, I exude a _____ energy!

One thing I've noticed over the years is that many people don't like their Rising Sign when they find it out. I suspect that's because many of us imagine we come across very differently to the way we actually do! You can find out more about your Rising Sign and what it means in the Astrological Cookbook in Chapter 13.

Remember that your Rising Sign (ascendant) is like the front door to your chart. The planet (or planets) that rules your Rising Sign is your overall chart's ruling planet(s). Once you advance in your astrological studies, you'll want to take a closer look at your Rising Signs' ruling planet(s), which are listed below:

The Rising Signs' ruling planets
Aries Rising: Mars is your ruling planet – read about Mars on page 57.

Taurus Rising: Venus is your ruling planet – read about Venus on page 55.

Gemini Rising: Mercury is your ruling planet – read about Mercury on page 53.

Cancer Rising: the Moon is your ruling planet – read about Moon on page 51.

Leo Rising: the Sun is your ruling planet – read about the Sun on page 49.

Virgo Rising: Mercury is your ruling planet – read about Mercury on page 53.

Libra Rising: Venus is your ruling planet – read about Venus on page 55.

Scorpio Rising: Mars and Pluto are your ruling planets – read about them on page(s) 57 and 67.

Sagittarius Rising: Jupiter is your ruling planet – read about Jupiter on page 59.

Capricorn Rising: Saturn is your ruling planet – read about Saturn on page 61.

Aquarius Rising: Saturn and Uranus are your ruling planets – read about them on pages 61 and 63.

Pisces Rising: Jupiter and Neptune are your ruling planets – read about them on pages 59 and 65.

The descendant (the Love Line)

This angle can be really interesting to look at because it's the one that rules the 7th house, aka the Love Zone. A person who has laid-back Sagittarius on his or her descendant will make a very different lover to someone who has, say, intense Scorpio.

Once you know a person's descendant (or Love Line as I like to call it), you have a much better idea of how and who they are in a relationship. That in itself gives you a good idea of what you can expect from them. This is useful information whether you're looking at a potential new lover, trying to make things better with your existing partner or even looking at a new friend or colleague.

There are various things you can pick up when you know which sign is on the descendant; for example, someone with Virgo on their descendant is going to be picky, while someone with Leo will want to be adored and he or she will be a generous lover. It can also describe the sort of lovers a person attracts, is attracted to, suits and stays with. For example, someone with Leo on their descendant wants a loud lover that he or she can show off, and someone with Gemini on their descendant could easily end up with a writer, someone who works in communications, or who indeed is a Gemini.

The easy way to work out someone's descendant or Love Line is to know their Rising Sign. Whatever that is, their Love Line is on the opposite side of the chart. Quite often, the Love Line will describe the person someone is attracted to. So someone with Capricorn on their Love Line could find people in uniform very attractive!

Below is a brief description for each sign on the Love Line (descendant).

Signs on the descendant

Aries descendant: traditionally wild and fiery and passionate. They're also spontaneous, to the point of being impulsive!

Taurus descendant: sensual and solid and usually pretty reliable. They want someone who will tickle their senses and preferably feed them.

Gemini descendant: they are adaptable, and will keep things both interesting and moving along in their relationships.

Cancer descendant: loving and comforting; however, they can be quite insecure and need a lot of reassurance.

Leo descendant: they want to be adored, even if they're quite quirky and act as if they don't need anyone or anything.

Virgo descendant: can be a tad picky; they prefer their partners to be extremely hygienic and often object to manufactured scents.

Libra descendant: these people make great partners. Guided by Venus, they are all about relationships without being clingy. They're often very big flirts.

Scorpio descendant: intense and passionate, these people want relationships they can throw themselves into.

Sagittarius descendant: these people are harder to pin down! They like someone who lets them do their own thing. They are adventurous and find foreigners attractive.

Capricorn descendant: these people are serious about their relationships. Even so, they may need to work a little harder to be warm and fuzzy if their partner needs it.

Aquarius descendant: these people make slightly aloof and detached lovers. That's not to say they aren't ardent, just very pragmatic.

Pisces descendant: these people look to their partner to bring some romance into their life. They can be slightly elusive, in a slippery fish kind of way.

Take it back to your birth chart

Make a note of the sign on your descendant.

My descendant (my Love Line) is in _____, therefore when I'm in a relationship, I exude a _____ energy.

The *Medium Coeli* (the MC, or Career Line)

The MC, or Career Line, tells you about a person's career, their professional life, their ambitions – what they are going to be known for. It speaks of their reputation.

Signs on the MC

Here's a brief description of the signs on the Career Line.

Aries on the MC: a career go-getter. Possibly a bit impetuous and can make rather professional moves.

Taurus on the MC: has the potential to do well financially. Looks after resources. Earthy. A reliable worker. Feminine.

Gemini on the MC: happy to do different jobs, to chop and change career direction; anything to do with words should work.

Cancer on the MC: could be a professional or full-time carer; they are caring and kind, if a little bit changeable, emotionally.

Leo on the MC: these people seek some kind of razzamatazz in their work; doing something a bit glamorous really works.

Virgo on the MC: a wonderful and reliable worker who will triple-check the facts and be happy to serve.

Libra on the MC: these people seek balanced careers doing something that's at the very least palatable, and preferably rather elegant.

Scorpio on the MC: doing research work or anything that requires some kind of digging; anything to do with sex or the occult suits.

Sagittarius on the MC: these people are freer and easier when it comes to their career. Anything to do with travel or publishing suits them really well. The self-employed person.

Capricorn on the MC: an excellent placement because Capricorn is nothing if not ambitious and ready to work hard.

Aquarius on the MC: these are the inventors and scientists; people who push the world forwards or work with technology. Good at self-employment.

Pisces on the MC: the dreamers of the career sphere. They want poetry, art or music in their jobs, if they can get it.

Take it back to your birth chart

Make a note of the sign on your MC.

My MC, or Career Line is in _____, therefore when I'm pursuing my ambitions, I exude a _____ energy.

The *Imum Coeli* (the IC, or Home Line)

The IC, or Home Line, represents the home: it's also the most private angle on the chart. What follows are some snapshot ideas to get you thinking about all the signs on the IC.

Signs on the IC

Aries on the IC: your challenge is to maintain harmony and equilibrium at home and with family.

Taurus on the IC: you know how to create a lovely home and a secure family feeling.

Gemini on the IC: you won't mind moving house/city/country over the course of your lifetime. Your home is a witty place to be!

Cancer on the IC: this is sort of the 'ideal', as Cancer is very home-y. Think feathered nest. Protectiveness.

Leo on the IC: you want your home to be a fun – not to mention gorgeous – place to be. You are very generous with family.

Virgo on the IC: your home is neat and tidy and you do all that you can to help your family members out, even if you're annoyed with them.

Libra on the IC: your home is beautiful and people like to be there because the energy is good. You can't bear family arguments.

Scorpio on the IC: your home may be dim and dark, with lots of soft lighting and velvet. You're private and intense about family.

Sagittarius on the IC: home is that place you come back to after you've been and done your wandering, cowboy/cowgirl.

Capricorn on the IC: home is organized and probably – and preferably – set somewhere old. There is an authoritarian air about it.

Aquarius on the IC: your personal life may be highly changeable or even chaotic. You love a high-tech home, or at least lots of gadgets and appliances.

Pisces on the IC: it may not always be 100 per cent clear where home is. Your family often inspires you. Your home is your spiritual base.

Take it back to your birth chart

Make a note of the sign on your MC.

My IC (or Home Line) is in _____, therefore when I'm at home and with my family, or in my private life, I exude a _____ energy.

Remember that every sign has an element too, which can influence it (see the information about the elements in Chapter 3). So a Water sign on the MC (or Career Line) would make you more likely to work with water or the emotions. Or at least you would find that satisfying, if you haven't already worked out how to make it happen.

People with a Fire sign on the MC want excitement at work. People with Earth want something steady, real, visceral and perhaps organic or alternative. People with an Air sign on the MC need mental stimulation. Can you see how it all starts to fit together?

Also note that if you find a planet in your chart that sits right on an angle, it will be a more important planet for you. The planet's characteristics (and of course the sign the planet and MC are in) lend a 'flavour' to that angle. For example, if you have Mars in Leo on your MC, your career or your approach to your career will have a Mars (driven) and Leo (razzle-dazzle) feel to it.

SUMMARY

You have now added one more layer to your understanding of a birth chart. Getting to know the four angles is crucial because they can give you an at-a-glance insight into a person when you see their birth chart. Do be aware that the angles need an accurate birth time in order to be accurate themselves.

Chapter 7
The houses

Next, you need to become more familiar with the 12 houses of astrology, which will allow you to really get to know your birth chart. Later in the book I'll be giving you an introduction to chart reading, a lot of which requires a good understanding of the 12 houses.

There are various different house systems in use in astrology, the most popular of which are probably Placidus, Equal and Whole Sign houses. In this book I've used Whole Sign houses, as I do in all my work, not least because super-astrologer Robert Hand uses and recommends them. Advocates of the Whole Signs system point out that Whole Sign houses are the oldest form of house division – they are thought to have originated around the 1st century BCE as part of the Greco-Roman tradition of astrology, Hellenistic astrology.

As you learned in Chapter 2, the zodiac (horoscope) is divided into 12 sections, or houses, each one ruled by a different sign – which sign rules which house in your chart depends on your Rising Sign. All the other signs follow on from the Rising Sign, going anticlockwise in the traditional order of Aries, Taurus, Gemini, Cancer, Leo, Virgo, Libra, Scorpio, Sagittarius, Capricorn, Aquarius and Pisces.

Each house is associated with a field of experience, beginning with the self, and expanding outwards into society and beyond. Within the houses are the planets. So you might have, for example, Mercury in Pisces in the 4th house.

When an astrologer interprets your chart, he or she blends the meaning of each planet, the house it's in, and the sign it's in, to understand the gifts and challenges, the talents, assets and obstacles you'll have in this lifetime. Unlike the elements and planets, houses are not 'energies', nor do they colour the expression of energies like the zodiac signs do. Instead, the houses are where these energies are most likely to manifest.

Different ways of looking at your birth chart

At the most fundamental level, the houses divide the birth chart into top and bottom.

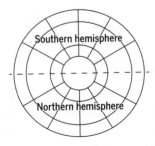

Figure 5: The houses North and South

The top half of the chart is the most visible part of our lives, while the lower half deals more with our private life. The top half of the chart is called the Southern Hemisphere (because the chart's perspective has us in it, looking out, so the North is ahead of us and the South is behind us). So a person with lots of planets in the top half of their chart lives their life quite openly – they are 'seen', they are out in society and they tend to be more outgoing and social.

Conversely, someone with lots of planets in the lower half of their chart (called the Northern Hemisphere), will be more private, perhaps more guarded, more subjective. They most likely prefer to keep themselves to themselves.

Astrologers also break the houses down into Eastern and Western hemispheres (as shown below). The line in the middle represents, and is sometimes called, the horizon.

Figure 6: The houses East and West

Again, the Eastern and Western divisions reflect the chart's perspective – with us on the inside, looking out. People who have more of their planets distinctly on the left, or Eastern, side of the chart tend to be more assertive – they show a lot of initiative, and are motivated self-starters. People with a lot more planets on the right of the chart, the Western side, are usually more oriented towards other people rather than self-focused. They ask less what you can do for them and more what they can do for you. They are often very thoughtful and considerate.

The 12 houses are also divided into four quadrants:

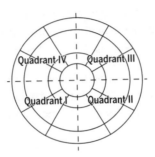

Figure 7: House quadrants

The houses in the first quadrant – houses 1, 2 and 3 – are all about self-awareness: where we discover our own personal identity. Those in the second quadrant – houses 4, 5 and 6 – are about self-expression: how we show the world who we are, and how we integrate with our environment.

The third quadrant – houses 7, 8 and 9 – is the area of self-expansion and social identity. It's about our awareness of others. The fourth quadrant – houses 10, 11 and 12 – is all about social expression and self-transcendence. It's about how we integrate with society.

Angular, succedent and cadent houses

The most important houses in the birth chart are often believed to be the 1st, 4th, 7th, and 10th houses. These are the angular houses, so named because their cusps coincide with the four angles: the ascendant, IC, descendant and MC. The planets in the angular houses may influence you the most.

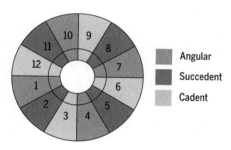

Figure 8: Angular, succedent and cadent houses

The houses that follow the angular houses in the birth chart are the succedent houses. The planets in the succedent houses are less powerful than those in the angular houses, but more powerful than those found in the third category, cadent houses. Succedent planets are effectively 'on the rise' – while the word 'cadent' means 'fallen' and is the root of the word cadaver, meaning corpse. Traditionally, planets here were regarded by astrologers as the weakest.

Note that the 11th house is seen as more powerful than other succedent houses and almost as strong as an angular house. It's known as the house of good fortune and good spirit.

House cusps

When you look at your chart, you'll see that a line separates each of the 12 houses – this is called the cusp or the house cusp. A house cusp is the imaginary dividing line between one house and another. For example, the 2nd house cusp is the dividing line between the 1st and 2nd houses – it's where the 2nd house starts. The 1st house cusp divides the 12th and 1st houses, and so on.

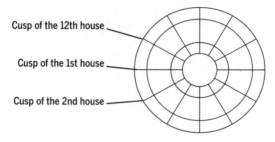

Cusp of the 12th house

Cusp of the 1st house

Cusp of the 2nd house

Figure 9: House 'cusps'

You may have heard the word 'cusp' before, in the phrase 'to be born on the cusp'. When astrologers talk about people being born on the cusp of a zodiac sign, it comes from the same idea of house cusps: they're referring to someone born on the changeover day when the Sun moves from one sign into another – usually between the 19th and 22nd of the month. Therefore you have the Sun passing over the house cusp.

There's a common misconception that being born 'on the cusp' makes you a bit of two signs. In fact, regardless of whether you were born on the cusp or not, your Sun (and indeed all planets and points) can only ever be one sign or another.

That changeover date varies from year to year, so if you were born on the cusp of a sign you'll need to find your definitive sign (if you haven't already done so). You can do this at theastrologybook.com/freechart. You are one sign or another and not a bit of both, even if you were born in the very first or last minute of your sign.

House cusp rulers

In Chapter 2, you identified the signs that rule the houses on your chart. The sign you have on each house is important because it casts a 'glow' over the whole house. Your ascendant, or Rising Sign, is the front door to your chart, so the sign you have on your ascendant is the sign that rules your 1st house.

This is important because the sign on your 1st house then dictates which sign is on your 2nd, 3rd and 4th houses, and so on. So if you're Scorpio Rising, say, moving one sign along the chart (remember that the signs go around anticlockwise in the order of Aries, Taurus, Gemini, Cancer, Leo, Virgo, Libra, Scorpio, Sagittarius, Capricorn, Aquarius and Pisces), means that Sagittarius rules your 2nd house, and you therefore spend and deal with the 2nd house issues of cash, property and possessions in a Sagittarian manner.

Your 3rd house would be ruled by the next sign, Capricorn. Since Capricorn is the sign of maturity and the 3rd house is your Communications Zone, you would communicate with Capricornian maturity. And so on.

Once you understand this, you can start to understand how people born on the same day but at different times can be so unalike. For example, someone born at 6 a.m. would be likely to have their Sun in their 12th house or their 1st house, whereas someone born on the same day at midday would be more likely to have it in their 9th or 10th house – the person with their Sun in the 12th or 1st house would be a very different character to the person with their Sun in the 9th or 10th house.

The meaning of the houses

What follows is a little more information about the part of life that each of the houses refers to or governs. As you read on, take a look at your own chart. The descriptions here are only the generic meaning of the house – what you also need to do, once you understand the meaning of each house in this sense, is add a layer of information with the characteristics of the sign that rules that house (see the *meaning of the signs* section on pages 75–93).

So for example, Aries ruling your 8th house (which governs sex and cash) will be very different to Virgo ruling your 8th house. If Aries rules your 8th house you'll express yourself sexually and in joint financial matters like an Aries – that is to say, with vim and vigour and drive and va va voom! Whereas if you have meeker and milder Virgo on your 8th house, you'll deal with the 8th house matters of sex and joint finances in a more detailed, careful, modest fashion.

The illustration opposite shows the areas covered by each house. This is something you'll start to remember automatically with practice, so look at it long and often.

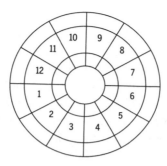

Figure 10: The 12 houses

House	Meaning
1	Your appearance and the way you come across, your social 'mask'
2	Cash, property, possessions and self-esteem, values, material wealth, what you value
3	Communications, siblings and neighbours, trips, transport, your mind
4	Home and family, where you feel you belong, emotional foundations, being settled
5	Romance, creativity and kids, fun, pregnancies, sex, flirting, risk-taking
6	Daily work, health and routines, being of service to others, alternative health, job situation
7	Partnerships (business and personal), one-to-one relationships, marriage, alliances, enemies
8	Birth, death, life's mysteries, rebirth, renewal, transformation, sex, joint finances
9	Travel, study and the Great Cosmic Quest, broadening the mind, gaining perspective
10	Your ambitions and career – how you make your mark, goals, public life, recognition
11	Friends, social circles, groups and clubs, wishes, spiritual aspirations
12	Self-sabotage, fear, your dreams, your inner self, secrets, self-transcendence, retreats, meditation, connection

1st house

Governs the way you come across – your image.

The 1st house is the initial impression that a person gives when we meet them. As you've seen, the 1st house is also the same sign as the Rising Sign; in fact, the Rising Sign dictates which sign is on the 1st house. Traditionally, astrologers have said that this house governs our physical appearance; personally, I'm not convinced by this. For me, it's far more about superficial appearance – our way of dressing and our style.

Regardless, this is the part of you that people see first when they see *you* coming. It's your business card, your website and your brand, rolled into one. Once you know which sign the 1st house is in, looking at the planet that rules that sign can be very educational. From this house, all the others flow.

2nd house

The domain of cash, property, possessions and self-esteem.

This is an awesome house, not least because it has a lot to teach us about the energetic connections between self-esteem and money. If you know anything about the Law of Attraction, you'll be aware that money pretty much manifests in direct relation to how highly we value ourselves, our talents, our services and what we have to offer the world.

This house, then, is about the material – it describes the financial condition and situation of a person's chart. It's also about what we hold dear, what we value. For example, are you a quick spender, good with money, or a little tight-fisted? It's a lot to do with your 2nd house: which sign rules it, which planets you were born with in there, and which planets are currently transiting it (more on this later).

3rd house

Governs communications, siblings and neighbours.

The 3rd house is first and foremost about communications. It's how a person listens, talks, and thinks. It's to do with everyday life – our neighbours, our siblings, the things we do automatically, and short trips. It's about letters and books and how you say things, as well as about why you say them. The sign on this house says a lot about how you sound when you speak (as does your Mercury). Do you come across as learned (Capricorn), or intuitive (Pisces), or caring (Cancer) or flippant (Sagittarius)?

Basic education comes into play in this part of the chart, too. This is the house you reason from. But most importantly, it's the part of your chart where you connect with others and talk to them or exchange with them. In some ways I think of the 3rd house as a really fun part of the chart, because it's the part where we have coffee with the neighbours and go on little outings and keep busy.

4th house

Rules home and family.

This is the part of the chart that's all about home and family; it's about where you feel you belong and the people who feel like family to you. The sign on the house goes a long way to showing what kind of family life you had in the past, and have today, and what sort of home you want to create. If there are family upsets and rifts to be healed, you can look at your 4th house for ideas of where the problems come from and how to fix them.

This house also denotes the womb, and is the 'cellar' of your chart – it's about the past and what you've stashed away, down in the cellar of your life (which is why family is also here... the people with whom you shared your past – those who helped shape you). It's about instinct and where you feel safe. Parents in general and the father specifically are also represented here.

5th house

The house of romance, creativity and kids.

Now we come to the Fun Zone of your chart. This is the part of you that's associated with romance, creativity and kids (your own or someone else's). It's your light-hearted side and what you do on the weekend. It's where you express yourself and even take some personal risks. It's the house of flirtation and good times. The sign on the house will show you how you have a good time.

The 5th house is all about love affairs too. Note that the 7th house is about deep love and relationships, which is different. The 5th house is about the chase and the seduction and the delights. It's about anything you love to do, too, and that includes being creative in any number of ways. Some people are creative in the kitchen, others with computer code. Hobbies come under this house, as do pleasure and fun.

6th house

Directs your daily work, health and routines.

Welcome to the house of work! The 6th house is where we do our daily grind and earn our daily bread. It's where we do things for other people and perform our work duties. It's the 'ticking over' part of your horoscope, not the most glamorous part, but very useful and practical. It's also about your routines – including your morning and evening routines and your self-care routines.

This is also the part of your chart that shows how well you do or don't look after yourself. As a result, the 6th house – traditionally the house of health – has a really alternative health feel: this is where you keep your inner physician, and if they're handy with a poultice, tincture or some Reiki, so much the better. Pets are also found in this house.

7th house

Refers to your lovers and your enemies.

Welcome to the house of love. Actually, it's the house of partnership as much as it is about love, but let's face it, the love aspect of the 7th house is pretty compelling. This is the house where you find the descendant (or Love Line). It's about the Other: the important other people in your life. That's often your beloved, your ex, or even people who are more like foes than friends but who loom large in your life. It can also show best friends, business partners and bosses. It's anyone who is a VIP in your life.

The 7th house is a bit like the 7th sign of Libra, and all about how we relate to other people. Me and you; me versus you;

I see me through your eyes. It can show our ideal self: the person we would love to be (as opposed to the ascendant, which shows how we come across, like it or not!). It's a 'you and them' place, and it's where you claim people as 'my boyfriend' or 'my husband'. The sign on this house can say a lot about the people you fall in love with. This is where we make commitments to the people we were only flirting with back in the 5th house.

8th house

This rules sex and other people's resources.

For me, this is a sinister house – if you go through ancient astrological manuscripts you'll find all manner of freaky writings about death. The 8th house was once the house of death, but these days we think of it in more enlightened terms: the house of death and rebirth, for instance. That brings a sort of Buddhist feeling into this otherwise slightly frightening domain. Think of it as the house where you have the phoenix rising from the ashes; the leaves that wither and disappear into the soil, only to be reabsorbed and later brought back to life when another plant flourishes there.

It's also about sex. Sex and death? Well, the French call sexual orgasm 'La petite mort' – the little death: go figure. The 8th house is about where we let go, which we also do in sex. It's funny, because this part of the horoscope is also traditionally about shared finances, such as credit card debts and salaries and even mortgages, which you might think go in the 4th house but actually live here. If you're doing a joint venture with someone, you're doing your 8th house. This is also the house of taboos: anything you don't like to talk about, like sex, death and taxes, goes here.

9th house

Governs travel, study and the Great Cosmic Quest To Understand Life.

This is the Adventure Zone in your chart. It's long-distance travel and where you go off on quests to discover the world. It's also the part of your chart where you go on cosmic quests, hoping to understand life and its mysteries. As a result, the 9th house is also associated with life philosophies.

It's also the Study Zone, when people move into higher education or broaden their mind in any way. This is the place in the chart where people see the proverbial Bigger Picture. For that reason, I also think of it as the 'Count Your Blessings Zone'. The sign on this house will give you an idea of your attitude to travel. It's also associated with legal matters.

10th house

Covers ambitions and career – how you make your mark.

This is the top point or pinnacle of your chart. The MC is the cusp of the 10th house in other house systems, but as we're using Whole Sign houses, the MC will float into other houses. It talks about what you came into this world to achieve and how you're going to attempt to pull that off. This should show how you'll make your mark and where you'll stand in society. Your status. Do you feel as if you were brought to this Earth to achieve great things? Look to your chart and your 10th house.

If someone wants to ask you about their professional life, look to their 10th house. How lofty are their ambitions? You can work that out by looking at this part of the chart. Which sign rules it? Which planets are in there? Many people are very at home with the 6th house, which is the part of the horoscope where the daily toil goes on. But the 10th house is where our career trajectory lies, and where we decide how ambitious we are. It's how we stand out and make our mark, even if we don't actually work a day in our lives. This house covers our reputation.

11th house

Governs friends, social circles and networks, and what you're wishing for.

This house is all about your friends, the social circles you move in and the social networks you belong to: and about how well you're connected on there. It's about the people you associate and hang out with. It's about the company you keep and the people who feel like kindred spirits. It's about being a part of a team, and how well you can fit in to that role. It's about your peers.

What kind of friend you are will show up in your 11th house. Do you learn lots of life lessons via your friends? If so, Saturn could rule or be in your 11th house. Do you really adore your friends and vice versa? Perhaps Venus is in your 11th house. Are friends your focus? You may have an 11th house Sun.

When this house is triggered (e.g. if there is a New or Full Moon, or a planet is in there and aspecting other planets), issues related to friends often come up. This part of the chart is also about your ideals – the things you aspire to. Hopefully you'll find friends who will be aspirational rather than a bad influence. And the 11th house is about what ye olde astrologers would call The Thing Wished For. In other words, this part of your chart is about what you're wishing for.

12th house

This is all about fears and spiritual life.

This is the part of your chart where you can withdraw, rest and retreat. It's the place you go when you've had enough and you need to refuel on energy or positive emotions. The planet and sign on the cusp of the 12th house will say a lot about how you do that. This is also, somewhat scarily, known as the house of self-sabotage, so be aware of that. Getting to know your 12th house will show you how you shoot yourself in the foot and how to stop doing that.

It's also the part of your chart where you keep a big connection to your spiritual life. Traditional astrologers won't agree, but many modern astrologers associate the 12th house with the planet of poetry and Divine connections, aka Neptune: the planet associated with Pisces since its discovery in 1846. For me, it's the deepest, darkest and most private part of your chart, and it's the place we tap into when we connect with the other dimensions. It may sometimes be associated with suffering and sacrifice, but it's also to do with the angels and guides who help us through tough times.

A guide to your house rulers

Once you know a person's ascendant (Rising Sign), it's easy to work out the rest of their houses, as all the zodiac signs follow in the traditional order in an anticlockwise direction. The sign that's on a house cusp flavours the matters related to that house.

So here's a guide to your houses – a quick way for you to work out which sign rules which house in your chart and what that means.

Aries or Aries Rising

❖ **Aries** rules your 1st house – you exude Aries energy.

❖ **Taurus** rules your 2nd house – you spend and save like a Taurean.

❖ **Gemini** rules your 3rd house – you think and communicate like a Gemini.

❖ **Cancer** rules your 4th house – your home and family life has a Cancerian flavour.

❖ **Leo** rules your 5th house – you have fun like a Leo.

❖ **Virgo** rules your 6th house – your daily life runs with a Virgoan flavour.

❖ **Libra** rules your 7th house – you relate like a Libran.

❖ **Scorpio** rules your 8th house – you spend and have sex like a Scorpio.

❖ **Sagittarius** rules your 9th house – you explore life like a Sagittarian.

❖ **Capricorn** rules your 10th house – professionally, you're like a Capricorn.

❖ **Aquarius** rules your 11th house – you're like an Aquarian with your friends.

❖ **Pisces** rules your 12th house – spiritually, you're very Piscean.

Taurus or Taurus Rising

❖ **Taurus** rules your 1st house – you exude Taurus energy.

❖ **Gemini** rules your 2nd house – you spend and save like a Gemini.

❖ **Cancer** rules your 3rd house – you think and communicate like a Cancerian.

❖ **Leo** rules your 4th house – your home and family life has a Leo flavour.

❖ **Virgo** rules your 5th house – you have fun like a Virgo.

❖ **Libra** rules your 6th house – your daily life runs with a Libran flavour.

❖ **Scorpi**o rules your 7th house – you love like a Scorpio.

❖ **Sagittarius** rules your 8th house – you spend and have sex like a Sagittarian.

❖ **Capricorn** rules your 9th house – you explore life like a Capricorn.

❖ **Aquarius** rules your 10th house – professionally, you're like an Aquarian.

❖ **Pisces** rules your 11th house – you're like a Piscean with your friends

❖ **Aries** rules your 12th house – spiritually, you're very Arian.

Gemini or Gemini Rising

❖ **Gemini** rules your 1st house – you exude Gemini energy.

❖ **Cancer** rules your 2nd house – you spend and save like a Cancerian.

❖ **Leo** rules your 3rd house – you think and communicate like a Leo.

❖ **Virgo** rules your 4th house – your home and family life has a Virgoan flavour.

❖ **Libra** rules your 5th house – you have fun like a Libran.

❖ **Scorpio** rules your 6th house – your daily life runs with a Scorpionic flavour.

❖ **Sagittarius** rules your 7th house – you love like a Sagittarian.

❖ **Capricorn** rules your 8th house – you spend and have sex like a Capricorn.

❖ **Aquarius** rules your 9th house – your explore life like an Aquarian.

❖ **Pisces** rules your 10th house – professionally, you're like a Piscean.

❖ **Aries** rules your 11th house – you're like an Aries with your friends.

❖ **Taurus** rules your 12th house – spiritually, you're very Taurean.

Cancer or Cancer Rising

❖ **Cancer** rules your 1st house – you exude Cancerian energy.

❖ **Leo** rules your 2nd house – you spend and save like a Leo.

❖ **Virgo** rules your 3rd house – you think and communicate like a Virgo.

❖ **Libra** rules your 4th house – your home and family life has a Cancerian flavour.

❖ **Scorpio** rules your 5th house – you have fun like a Scorpio.

❖ **Sagittarius** rules your 6th house – your daily life runs with a Sagittarian flavour.

❖ **Capricorn** rules your 7th house – you love like a Capricorn.

❖ **Aquarius** rules your 8th house – you spend and have sex like an Aquarian.

❖ **Pisces** rules your 9th house – you explore life like a Piscean.

❖ **Aries** rules your 10th house – professionally, you're like an Aries.

❖ **Taurus** rules your 11th house – you're like a Taurean with your friends.

❖ **Gemini** rules your 12th house – spiritually, you're very Gemini.

Leo or Leo Rising

❖ **Leo** rules your 1st house – you exude Leo energy.

❖ **Virgo** rules your 2nd house – you spend and save like a Virgo.

❖ **Libra** rules your 3rd house – you think and communicate like a Libran.

❖ **Scorpio** rules your 4th house – your home and family life has a Scorpio flavour.

- ❖ **Sagittarius** rules your 5th house – you have fun like a Sagittarius.

- ❖ **Capricorn** rules your 6th house – your daily life runs with a Capricorn flavour.

- ❖ **Aquarius** rules your 7th house – you love like an Aquarian.

- ❖ **Pisces** rules your 8th house – you spend and have sex like a Piscean.

- ❖ **Aries** rules your 9th house – you explore life like an Aries.

- ❖ **Taurus** rules your 10th house – professionally, you're like a Taurean.

- ❖ **Gemini** rules your 11th house – you're like a Gemini with your friends.

- ❖ **Cancer** rules your 12th house – spiritually, you're very Cancerian.

Virgo or Virgo Rising

- ❖ **Virgo** rules your 1st house – you exude Virgo energy.

- ❖ **Libra** rules your 2nd house – you spend and save like a Libran.

- ❖ **Scorpio** rules your 3rd house – you think and communicate like a Scorpio.

- ❖ **Sagittarius** rules your 4th house – your home and family life has a Sagittarian flavour.

- ❖ **Capricorn** rules your 5th house – you have fun like a Sagittarius.

- ❖ **Aquarius** rules your 6th house – your daily life runs with an Aquarian flavour.

❖ **Pisces** rules your 7th house – you love like a Piscean.

❖ **Aries** rules your 8th house – you spend and have sex like an Aries.

❖ **Taurus** rules your 9th house – you explore life like a Taurean.

❖ **Gemini** rules your 10th house – professionally, you're like a Gemini.

❖ **Cancer** rules your 11th house – you're like a Cancerian with your friends.

❖ **Leo** rules your 12th house – spiritually, you're very Leonine.

Libra or Libra Rising

❖ **Libra** rules your 1st house – you exude Libra energy.

❖ **Scorpio** rules your 2nd house – you spend and save like a Scorpio.

❖ **Sagittarius** rules your 3rd house – you think and communicate like a Sagittarius.

❖ **Capricorn** rules your 4th house – your home and family life has an Aquarian flavour.

❖ **Aquarius** rules your 5th house – you have fun like an Aquarian.

❖ **Pisces** rules your 6th house – your daily life runs with a Piscean flavour.

❖ **Aries** rules your 7th house – you love like an Aries.

❖ **Taurus** rules your 8th house – you spend and have sex like a Taurean.

- ❖ **Gemini** rules your 9th house – you explore life like a Gemini.

- ❖ **Cancer** rules your 10th house – professionally, you're very Cancerian.

- ❖ **Leo** rules your 11th house – you're like a Leo with your friends.

- ❖ **Virgo** rules your 12th house – spiritually, you're very Virgoan.

Scorpio or Scorpio Rising

- ❖ **Scorpio** rules your 1st house – you exude Scorpio energy.

- ❖ **Sagittarius** rules your 2nd house – you spend and save like a Sagittarius.

- ❖ **Capricorn** rules your 3rd house – you think and communicate like a Capricorn.

- ❖ **Aquarius** rules your 4th house – your home and family life has an Aquarian flavour.

- ❖ **Pisces** rules your 5th house – you have fun like a Piscean.

- ❖ **Aries** rules your 6th house – your daily life runs with an Aries flavour.

- ❖ **Taurus** rules your 7th house – you love like a Taurean.

- ❖ **Gemini** rules your 8th house – you spend and have sex like a Gemini.

- ❖ **Cancer** rules your 9th house – you explore life like a Cancerian.

- ❖ **Leo** rules your 10th house – professionally, you're very Leo.

❖ **Virgo** rules your 11th house – you're like a Virgo with your friends.

❖ **Libra** rules your 12th house – spiritually, you're very Libran.

Sagittarius or Sagittarius Rising

❖ **Sagittarius** rules your 1st house – you exude Sagittarian energy.

❖ **Capricorn** rules your 2nd house – you save and spend like a Capricorn.

❖ **Aquarius** rules your 3rd house – you think and communicate like an Aquarian.

❖ **Pisces** rules your 4th house – your home and family life has a Piscean flavour.

❖ **Aries** rules your 5th house – you have fun like an Aries.

❖ **Taurus** rules your 6th house – your daily life runs with a Taurean flavour.

❖ **Gemini** rules your 7th house – you love like a Gemini.

❖ **Cancer** rules your 8th house – you spend and have sex like a Cancerian.

❖ **Leo** rules your 9th house – you explore life like a Leo.

❖ **Virgo** rules your 10th house – professionally, you're very Virgoan.

❖ **Libra** rules your 11th house – you're like a Libran with your friends.

❖ **Scorpio** rules your 12th house – spiritually, you're very Scorpio.

Capricorn or Capricorn Rising

❖ **Capricorn** rules your 1st house – you exude Capricornian energy.

❖ **Aquarius** rules your 2nd house – you spend and save like an Aquarian.

❖ **Pisces** rules your 3rd house – you think and communicate like a Piscean.

❖ **Aries** rules your 4th house – your home and family life has an Aries flavour.

❖ **Taurus** rules your 5th house – you have fun like a Taurean.

❖ **Gemini** rules your 6th house – your daily life has a Gemini flavour.

❖ **Cancer** rules your 7th house – you love like a Cancerian.

❖ **Leo** rules your 8th house – you spend and have sex like a Leo.

❖ **Virgo** rules your 9th house – you explore life like a Virgo.

❖ **Libra** rules your 10th house – professionally, you're very Libran.

❖ **Scorpio** rules your 11th house – you're like a Scorpio with your friends.

❖ **Sagittarius** rules your 12th house – spiritually, you're very Sagittarian.

Aquarius or Aquarius Rising

❖ **Aquarius** rules your 1st house – you exude Aquarian energy.

❖ **Pisces** rules your 2nd house – you spend and save like a Piscean.

❖ **Aries** rules your 3rd house – you think and communicate like an Aries.

❖ **Taurus** rules your 4th house – your home and family life has a Taurean flavour.

❖ **Gemini** rules your 5th house – you have fun like a Gemini.

❖ **Cancer** rules your 6th house – your daily life runs with a Cancerian flavour.

❖ **Leo** rules your 7th house – you love like a Leo.

❖ **Virgo** rules your 8th house – you spend and have sex like a Virgo.

❖ **Libra** rules your 9th house – you explore life like a Libran.

❖ **Scorpio** rules your 10th house – professionally, you're very Scorpionic.

❖ **Sagittarius** rules your 11th house – you're like a Sagittarian with your friends.

❖ **Pisces** rules your 12th house – spiritually, you're very Piscean.

Pisces or Pisces Rising

❖ **Pisces** rules your 1st house – you exude Piscean energy.

❖ **Aries** rules your 2nd house – you spend and save like an Aries.

❖ **Taurus** rules your 3rd house – you think and communicate like a Taurean.

- ❖ **Gemini** rules your 4th house – your home and family life has a Gemini flavour.

- ❖ **Cancer** rules your 5th house – you have fun like a Cancerian.

- ❖ **Leo** rules your 6th house – your daily life runs with a Leo flavour.

- ❖ **Virgo** rules your 7th house – you love like a Virgo.

- ❖ **Libra** rules your 8th house – you spend and have sex like a Libran.

- ❖ **Scorpio** rules your 9th house – you explore life like a Scorpio.

- ❖ **Sagittarius** rules your 10th house – professionally, you're very Sagittarian.

- ❖ **Capricorn** rules your 11th house – you're like a Capricorn with your friends.

- ❖ **Aquarius** rules your 12th house – spiritually, you're very Aquarian.

Take it back to your birth chart

Make a note of which houses your planets are in.

Go through your chart and see which planet is in which house, then memorize the information below on how this plays out in your life.

My Sun is in my _____ house. This is where I shine.

My Moon is in my _____ house. This is what I need.

My Mercury is in my _____ house. This is what's on my mind a lot.

My Venus is in my _____ house. This is what I love.

My Mars is in my _____ house. This is where I fight.

My Jupiter is in my _____ house. This is where I'm luckier.

My Saturn is in my _____ house. This is where my lessons come from.

My Uranus is in my _____ house. This is where I'm subject to change.

My Neptune is in my _____ house. This is where I'm inspired, or where I may wear blinkers.

My Pluto is in my _____ house. This is where I'm ripe for transformation.

SUMMARY

In this chapter, we've delved into deeper astrology via the 12 houses. You've now learned about the divisions of the horoscope and how important the houses are. You know that the 12 houses are divided into three subsections of angular, succedent and cadent. Plus, you've seen what each house means. You've also learned about the importance of checking to see which sign is on which house. This is all vital information for you to take in and work with.

Part II
GOING DEEPER

Chapter 8
Degrees, aspects and orbs

If you look at the printout of your chart, in the top right corner you'll find a table that shows the planetary glyphs with numbers next to them. Those numbers tell you the exact degree of the sign a planet was located in the heavens at the moment of your birth.

The degrees – which are taken from an astronomical almanac called an ephemeris (see page 247) – are crucial for gaining a deeper understanding of a birth chart. But unfortunately, they are also where many people stop short in their studies, thinking they are too complicated and 'mathematical'.

Don't be one of those people! I'm far from being a maths major, but these days with computers, understanding degrees is really nothing to do with understanding maths. Let's go at this very simply.

Identifying the degrees in your chart

As you know, in Western astrology horoscope charts are drawn as circles. There are 360 degrees in a circle, and the chart is divided into 12 equal sections (the signs and houses).

Each of those sections therefore contains 30 degrees, so each sign has 30 degrees in it. (Note that in astrology, we go from 0 to 29 degrees, not 1–30.)

Each degree also has 0–59 minutes and seconds. So it goes from 00.00 of a sign to 29.59 of a sign. (Remember that we always go anticlockwise when looking at a chart, including when counting degrees.) Here's an example that resembles those you'll see in the table on your chart:

$$\odot \ 14°\ 23'\ 33''\ ♈$$

This is the Sun (at) 14 degrees and 23 minutes and 33 seconds (of) Aries.

Note that each of the 360 degrees potentially has a planet or cusp or other point on it.

Take it back to your birth chart

Make a note of which planet sits at which degree in your chart.

Use the table on your chart to complete the following (here, we won't include the seconds):

My Sun is at _____ degrees and _____ minutes of _____ (sign)

My Moon is at _____ degrees and _____ minutes of _____ (sign)

My ascendant is at _____ degrees and _____ minutes of _____ (sign)

My Mercury is at _____ degrees and _____ minutes of _____ (sign)

My Venus is at _____ degrees and _____ minutes of
_____ (sign)

My Mars is at _____ degrees and _____ minutes of
_____ (sign)

My Jupiter is at _____ degrees and _____ minutes of
_____ (sign)

My Saturn is at _____ degrees and _____ minutes of
_____ (sign)

My Uranus is at _____ degrees and _____ minutes of
_____ (sign)

My Neptune is at _____ degrees and _____ minutes of
_____ (sign)

My Pluto is at _____ degrees and _____ minutes of
_____ (sign)

Why calculate the degrees?

The main purpose of working out the degrees is to do the
following:

1. Calculate the angles – known as aspects – that the
   planets are making to each other in your chart: how they
   join up, from one part of your chart to another, or indeed
   from the same part of your chart to another (in the case
   of what's called a conjunction – see below).

2. Measure the angles (aspects) that the transiting planets
   (the planets in the sky right now) are making to your
   chart (or someone else's).

3. Find out how someone else's planets aspect your
   planets when you're investigating compatibility.

4. Measure how the transiting planets are aspecting each other, if you want to get a sense of what's going on in the skies right now.

So what are the angles, or aspects?

Planetary aspects (aka planetary angles)

An aspect – or angle – between two planets is a connection between them. It's deduced by looking at the degrees. So for example, if you have a planet at 15 degrees of a Fire or Air sign, and another planet at around 15 degrees (allow 5 degrees either side) of a Fire or Air sign, they are said to be in *easy*, or harmonious aspect. (Fire and Fire, and Air and Air, and Fire and Air go together). It's the same if you have planets within 5 degrees of each other in Earth or Water signs. These would also be in easy (harmonious) aspect to each other.

However, if you have one or more planets at 23 degrees of a Water sign, say, and you also have one planet or more at around 23 degrees (give or take 5 degrees) of a Fire or Air sign, those planets are said to be in a *challenging* aspect to each other.

Aspects are hugely important in chart interpretation. They show how the planetary and sign energies play out. From the aspect two planets make to each other (or the aspects planets make to the four angles of the chart) we can see, among other things, whether there will be challenges or whether things will flow easily (be harmonious). Without understanding degrees and aspects, you'll never fully understand your own chart or anyone else's.

Conjunctions, sextiles, squares, trines and oppositions

There are five main aspects used in basic astrology: conjunctions, sextiles, squares, trines and oppositions. That said, this is a kind of shorthand, because the word aspect means 'view'. Technically, a conjunction isn't an aspect, because two planets standing side by side can't view each other. So really, we should say 'conjunctions and aspects', though a conjunction is treated as an aspect.

If you look at the centre circle of your chart, you'll see lines running between the planets. On them sit the glyphs for the aspects; as with the other points on the chart – the signs and planets – they are represented by symbols. The table below shows the glyphs for the aspects and how many degrees apart planets and points need to be from each other to form those aspects.

Aspect name	Glyph	Degrees apart
Conjunction	☌	0 degrees
Sextile	⚹	60 degrees
Square	☐	90 degrees
Trine	△	120 degrees
Opposition	☍	180 degrees

Try to locate the aspects on your chart: you may find all five of them there, or just a few.

You can calculate the aspects by looking at the degree the planet is at.

❖ If there's a planet right next to it (same or within 5 degrees), it's a conjunction.

❖ If there's a planet around the same degree two signs away in either direction, that's a sextile.

❖ If there's a planet around the same degree three signs away in either direction, that's a square.

❖ If there's a planet around the same degree four signs away in either direction, that's a trine.

❖ If there's a planet around the same degree opposite, that's an opposition.

You can also verify the aspects on your chart by counting the degrees.

Now look at the grid under your birth chart: there you can see at a glance which aspects your planets are making to other planets.

Below is a description of the five aspects, along with their glyphs. There's also another word to learn before we go further – orb, which means 'range of degrees'.

Conjunction ♂
This means two or more planets are in the same place or on the same degree (with an 8-degree orb, unless the Sun and/ or Moon are involved, in which case allow a 10-degree orb). For example, one planet at 22 degrees of Leo and one at 26 degrees of Leo would be said to be conjunct or conjoined. Planets can also be conjoined in different signs.

Conjunctions are easy or challenging depending on which planets are involved. For example a conjunction between the Sun and Venus is likely to be easy whereas a conjunction between Venus and Saturn could be more challenging. However, we need to keep an open mind as these can go either way.

Sextile ✶

This aspect is when planets are 60 degrees apart (in either direction). In other words, when they are two signs apart and on the same degree, give or take 5 degrees (or 6 if the Sun and/or Moon are involved).

Sextiles are easy aspects. The energy between the planets flows. Sextiles are productive and dynamic.

Square ☐

This aspect is when planets are 90 degrees apart (in either direction). In other words, when they are three signs apart and on the same degree, give or take 5 degrees (or 10 if the Sun and/or Moon are involved). Note that a square is half an opposition (see below).

Squares are challenging aspects, bringing a clash between the planets involved. However, they irritate enough to bring about change.

Trine △

This is when the planets are 120 degrees apart (in either direction). In other words, when they are four signs apart and on the same degree, give or take 5 degrees (or 10 if the Sun and/or Moon are involved).

Trines are easy, flowing aspects, and the planets involved are in harmony. They can, however, breed complacency.

Opposition ☍

This is when planets are 180 degrees apart – i.e. on opposite sides of the chart from each other and on the same degree, give or take 5 degrees (or 10 if the Sun and/or Moon are involved).

Oppositions are generally challenging aspects; however, note that oppositional planets are always in compatible elements. Fire signs are always opposite Air signs, and Earth signs are always opposite Water signs. So sometimes you get a clash and sometimes you get something that works well. Remember: opposites can attract! Also they bring out both sides of the issues indicated by the planets involved and that can be a very good thing.

To see if you're getting the hang of the degrees and aspect, try answering the question below (remember: there are 30 degrees in a sign and 12 signs).

Question: If your Sun is at 12 Gemini and your Venus is at 12 Leo (two signs later), how many degrees apart are they?

Hint: go through the signs in the traditional order of Aries, Taurus, Gemini, Cancer, Leo, Virgo, Libra, Scorpio, Sagittarius, Capricorn, Aquarius and Pisces to get your answer.

Answer: your Sun and Venus would be 60 degrees apart. This is a sextile aspect.

The condition of a planet

Sometimes you'll hear astrologers talking about a planet's 'condition' – in other words, what kind of state or condition it's in. Traditionally that would refer to its dignity, as judged by the table of dignities (see page 265). More colloquially though, a major influence on a planet's condition is which aspects it's making to other planets. Is it in harmony (making sextiles and trines) to the other planets or is it challenged (making squares and oppositions)?

As explained above, the harmonious (easy) aspects are trines and sextiles. So when you have planets in trine or sextile aspect to each other on your chart, you'll know they are in pretty good condition because these aspects suggest an easy flow between the planets – they are not challenged but rather in harmony.

We saw earlier that Fire and Air, and Earth and Water, go together – if you look at your chart and count a sextile's 60 degrees (two signs) and a trine's 120 degrees (four signs), you'll see that the Fire/Air and Earth/Water rules apply. Planets in compatible elements (i.e. Fire, Earth, Air and Water) make sextiles and trines to each to other, while planets in incompatible elements makes squares.

The most challenging aspect is the square – they cause a discomfort or a rawness or roughness that in my opinion is visceral. If you have planets squaring each other, they cause each other issues that tend to be sore points, and opportunities from which you can learn. With a square, a problem comes up that you have to do something about. It's an itch that must be scratched and from that point of view, squares are good aspects because they force us to deal with things and hopefully evolve.

Conjunctions and oppositions can go either way, depending on the planets involved, as explained earlier.

Remember, there are different ways that aspects can be made:

❖ The aspects your planets make to each other in your chart.

❖ The aspects that the planets up in the sky right now, moving around or 'transiting', make to the planets in your chart. I'll explain more about this in Chapter 15.

❖ You can also look at the aspects that the transiting planets make to each other, if you want to get a feeling of what is going on energetically in the world.

Interpreting the aspects

In addition, some planets are easier than others and that affects our interpretation of the aspects (see *The meaning of the planets* section on pages 48–68).

So Moon (feelings) square Venus (love) would be a lighter energy than, say, Venus (love) square Saturn (heavy-duty karma). As soon as Mars and Saturn or the planets beyond get involved, you're in heavier, more intense energy.

Another way to think of it is to substitute the words 'sextile' or 'trine' with 'is in harmony with' and to substitute the words 'square' or 'opposition' with 'is clashing with'. For example, Venus square Pluto then becomes Venus is clashing with Pluto. Mercury trine Jupiter becomes Mercury is in harmony with Jupiter.

To interpret Venus square Pluto in your chart, you would think about the following:

1. What does the planet Venus represent? Love, money, lessons?

2. Which sign is Venus in? (The sign's meaning helps you to understand it better.)

3. Which house is it in? (The house's meaning adds another layer of information.)

4. What does the planet Pluto represent? Power, transformation, obsession?

5. Which sign is Pluto in?

6. Which house is it in?

On a birth chart, a planet won't really be able to exude at full power if, say, it's squared by an aspect from Mars (angry), Saturn (depressive), Uranus (chaotic), Neptune (confusing) or Pluto (volcanic rebirther). So if someone with Venus in Gemini – who you'd expect to be terribly chatty and upbeat – has their Venus squared by bulldozer Saturn, they may not exhibit as much of the full-blown Gemini magic as someone with a Venus trined by Jupiter. Do you get the picture?

Here's another example: someone with their love planet Venus in a harmonious aspect (sextile or trine) to Jupiter (a happy planet) is going to have a very different Venus to someone with their Venus clashing with (squaring or opposing) volcanic Pluto.

There is a subtlety you need to come to grips with as you work with aspects. No planet is innately good or bad. However, if a planet is clashing with another, then the more negative traits of those planets are likely to come out. If two planets are in harmony (sextiling or trining), you get the best they have to offer.

Remember: when a planet sextiles or trines another planet, the energies flow. When they square or oppose, there is a clash.

There are 90 possible basic aspects, and interpretations of what exactly each of them means have filled entire books. However, I recommend you read one in particular to further your studies beyond the scope of this book: Sue Tompkin's *Aspects In Astrology*.

Unaspected planets

Some planets will not have links to other planets within orb. In other words, they aren't making any aspects at all to other planets. In that case, they are called 'unaspected'. This means they function on their own rather than forever in tandem with one or more other planets. The general consensus is that unaspected planets run their own story: they march to the beat of their own drum, and they do their own thing.

Also note that a person with an unaspected Sun in particular tends to be very unusual in some way – a maverick, someone who lives outside of the restrictions and norms the rest of us more or less conform to. It doesn't make them totally wacky; rather, it just ups their 'different' quotient a fair bit. They are often the people who think outside the proverbial square.

If you're still unclear about degrees and aspects, you'll find a video that explains them visually at theastrologybook.com/degreesaspects

SUMMARY

Congratulations! You are officially on your way to becoming a proper astrologer. The main thing is to know the signs and planets and then get to the degrees and aspects – but *do* get to them, because they are the cherry on the top of the astrology cake.

For now, it's enough to consider the following when looking at the aspects on your chart, or that of a friend or family member:

❖ **Conjuctions** can be easy *or* challenging, depending on which planets are conjoining. For example, Saturn on your Sun could well be harder to handle than, say, Jupiter on your Sun.

❖ **Trines and sextiles** are easier. They mix the energies harmoniously. Everyone is happy. So Venus trine Jupiter is lovely because Venus and Jupiter are already very pleasing planets and when you put them together in a pleasing angle, you double your pleasure potential. Even Venus trine Saturn or Saturn trine Pluto is positive, despite the fact that Saturn and Pluto can both be so challenging individually.

❖ **Squares and oppositions** are more challenging. So the Sun square Mars will bring out the more negative sides of the two planets – for example, the Sun's egotistical side and Mars's angry side.

Chapter 9
Aspect and chart patterns

Next we're going to take a brief look at some of the patterns and shapes that the planets make in a birth chart. This will give you even more information about how the planets are playing out in your chart. When three or more planets are connected to each other by aspect, they form a pattern. Understanding these patterns will build on the information you've already absorbed regarding the five basic aspects; for example, you know now that a square is challenging, but a T-square aspect pattern is even more challenging!

Major aspect patterns

The Grand Trine, T-Square, Yod and Kite are some of the major aspect patterns, so let's explore these.

The T-square

This is when you have two planets in opposition with a planet 'in the middle' of the two opposing planets, squaring both. See the illustration on the following page. One square is challenging but in the T-square there are not one but two squares and an opposition. There is push and shove with the T-square.

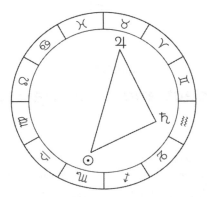

Figure 11: The T-square

Take it back to your birth chart

If you have a T-square in your chart, take a look at all the factors involved – the planets, signs and houses. These will help you to build up a picture of the issues likely to come up for you.

The Grand Trine

Here, three planets are connected by three trines to form a triangle, the Grand Trine.

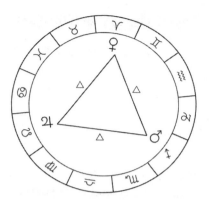

Figure 12: The Grand Trine

The Grand Trine shows flowing energies that go from one to the next. This aspect pattern reminds me of people holding hands and sending love around a circle. Any planetary influences in a Grand Trine circulate easily: in fact, sometimes too easily.

There are four different types of Grand Trine – one for each element.

❖ **Fire Grand Trine**: things are going well, and things are getting done because of enthusiasm.

❖ **Earth Grand Trine**: things can flow well when a practical approach is taken.

❖ **Air Grand Trine**: ideas and intellectualism will get things flowing.

❖ **Water Grand Trine**: people's feelings are flowing and there's compassion involved.

Take it back to your birth chart

Can you see a Grand Trine in your chart? Grand Trines can be where you are a little on the lazy side! Overall though, I would consider a Grand Trine a blessing.

The Yod

This is a rare aspect between three planets, or other points, that form a triangle. Two planets are sextile and the third is quincunx (150 degrees apart), on their midpoint.

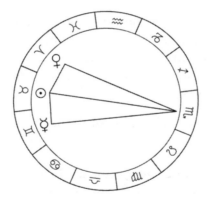

Figure 13: The Yod

Many say that the Yod suggests a special mission or destiny in life, and for this reason it's also called the Finger of God. However, others argue it's not all that informative. I would argue that we all come to Earth with a special mission or destiny, and that we don't need a Yod in our charts for that.

Take it back to your birth chart

Can you see a Yod in your chart? At its best, a Yod may challenge you to move from what is easy (sextile) to something far more awkward (quincunx) to live out your special mission.

The Mystic Rectangle

The wonderful-sounding Mystic Rectangle occurs when four or more planets are connected by sextiles, trines and oppositions.

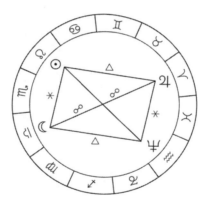

Figure 14: The Mystic Rectangle

The Mystic Rectangle allows the individual to work well in life, in whatever field they choose, personally and professionally. There is an energy flow.

Is there a Mystic Rectangle in your chart? This pattern is said to confer psychic ability, and it offers a strong sense of balance and harmony between the four planets involved.

The Kite

A Kite is a Grand Trine with a fourth planet opposing one of the three planets in the Grand Trine and sextiling the other two.

Figure 15: The Kite

The Opposition here is like the grit in the oyster that creates the pearl. On its own, a Grand Trine can be pleasant but it may not lead to grand and concrete developments. The Opposition gives the individual a sense of direction and focus and acts like an anchor for all that's good about the Grand Trine.

Take it back to your birth chart

Can you see a Kite in your chart? This pattern adds tension to your chart, and helps you to make the most of the positive energies it contains.

Major chart patterns

Once you've taken a good look at your chart, you may notice that you have a lot of planets in one place or large empty sections. What follows is a brief look at how to interpret the various patterns you might see.

See-saw

When the planets are laid out in the chart in two opposing groups, it suggests that there are lots of 'opposites' in the individual, perhaps playing out as contradictions. With this pattern, there's often a sort of see-sawing between one way of being and another.

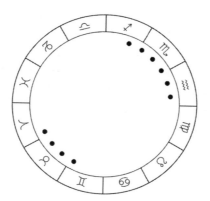

Figure 16: The see-saw

Tripod/splay

Here, the planets are in tight groups of three or four. This has the effect of highlighting several houses, which may become the most important houses (or areas of interest) in the individual's life.

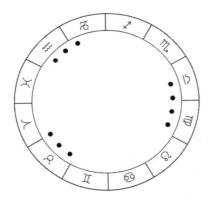

Figure 17: The tripod/splay

Locomotive

In this pattern, all the planets are bunched together and take up two-thirds of the chart, leaving one third, or 120 degrees, empty. This suggests a certain emphasis on one part of the chart, whereas the other part of the chart, where there are no planets, is less of a focus.

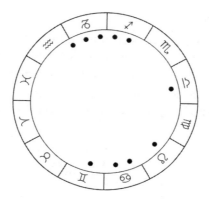

Figure 18: The locomotive

Bucket

This is when all the planets in the chart are on one side, except for the 'singleton' on the other side. The singleton becomes a very important planet in the chart of the person with this layout, both in terms of how it's expressed in the birth chart and what happens when it's transited by other planets.

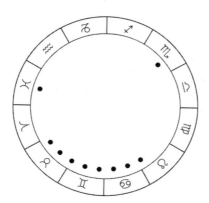

Figure 19: The bucket

Bundle/wedge

Here, the planets are gathered together within 120 degrees of each other. This confers areas of special interest. If you have a lot of planets in one particular part of your chart, your focus in this lifetime will be on those areas, taking into account the sign and house the bundle or wedge is in.

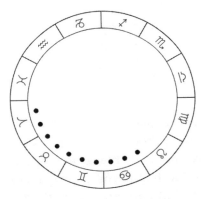

Figure 20: The bundle or wedge

Splash

This is when the planets are evenly spread out around the zodiac/chart. The individual has a wide range of gifts and abilities; however, they also need to focus on one thing at a time to achieve their goals.

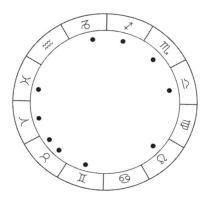

Figure 21: The splash

You should now have an understanding of the main chart patterns to look for when viewing your own or someone else's chart.

Once you start to look at charts more regularly, you may find that the patterns start to jump out at you rather quickly. They are a sort of visual shorthand and carry a lot of clues about the chart's overall character.

Next we will look at something even many non-astrologers have heard of – retrograde planets. If you have ever wondered about Mercury retrograde or the meaning of any other planet's retrograde, read on!

Chapter 10
Retrograde planets

Now we come to a part of astrology you've probably already heard of. All of the planets – with the exception of the Sun and Moon, which as you know, are actually luminaries, not planets – do something called 'going retrograde' from time to time. A retrograde is an apparent motion in which a planet 'appears' to move backwards in the sky (although none of the planets actually do move backwards as they orbit the Sun).

What causes a retrograde?

The reason why planets appear to move backwards is most easily explained as follows. Imagine you're on a train and outside the window, a little way ahead, you see a woman riding a horse. She's going fast, but the train is going faster. So the train keeps moving and you start to catch up with the woman on the horse. Eventually, you are about neck and neck with her. Then, as the train moves past the woman and the horse, they appear to move backwards, from where you are sitting.

This is how retrogrades work from our vantage point. The Earth sees Mercury ahead, for example, but the Earth moves faster than Mercury, so as we catch up and then overtake that planet, Mercury appears to go backwards.

You'll know that Venus or Mercury are about to turn retrograde when you see them move far ahead of the Sun in the ephemeris or the night sky. Mercury turns retrograde when it's about 14 degrees ahead of the Sun, and Venus turns retrograde when it's about 30 degrees ahead of the Sun.

This means that instead of progressing forwards through the zodiac, from one sign to another, Mercury actually appears to be going backwards through whatever sign it was in when the retrograde started. It's an illusion, but a meaningful one, symbolically!

How do planet retrogrades affect us?

When a planet goes retrograde, we get a stalling in the proceeding of that planet. (You can find out when the planets go retrograde by reading an ephemeris – see pages 247–249 or by keeping an eye on astrological websites. Retrograde planets are marked with the glyph that looks like an Rx.) It's a time when instead of pushing relentlessly forwards, as we tend to do in the modern world, we get a chance to take a breather. It's also a time when the energies get turned in on themselves.

If a planet is in retrograde on your birth chart, you'll feel the energy of that planet in a deeper, more internal way. In general, a retrograde planet in your chart can mean the energies are turned in on themselves, turned upside down somehow, or more introspective. When a planet is retrograde, it can be shy and a bit awkward. But it can also possess great depth. It may lack confidence but it will be highly sensitive.

Obviously, if you happened to have been born when there was a retrograde going on, you'll have that planet retrograde on your birth chart. You'll see it on your chart, marked with this symbol: ℞ (see below). You may be wondering whether retrogrades are bad luck? Not at all – everything happens for a reason, including planets going backwards. Retrogrades are neither good nor bad.

The meaning of retrogrades

As you know, each planet has its own unique cycle when it comes to orbiting the Sun, and it also has its own frequency and duration of retrogrades. The way a retrograde affects a person varies, depending on his or her birth chart. However, the descriptions below reveal the main themes of all the planets in retrograde (rx for short).

To see if you have any planets retrograde on your chart, look at the list of planets and degrees at the top right of your birth chart. Retrograde planets are marked with a red ℞ – an R with its tail crossed. In medicine, this symbol is used to mean 'prescription'; it's from the Latin word *recipere*, in its imperative form, meaning 'to take back'. The planet involved is being taken back.

Mercury retrograde

Mercury retrograde is perhaps the best known of all retrogrades, and you've probably heard of it. It happens up to four times a year. Mercury is the communications planet so when it reverses, communications can go awry. However, there's more to Mercury retrograde than that. For one thing, it's a chance to rethink and revisit and re-edit and revise. We all need to do that from time to time.

So don't wish Mercury retrogrades away; instead, look and see where they are taking place in your chart (in which house and over which of your planets) and work consciously with the energies. To do that, work out which sign and house the retrograde is taking place in and think about how that part of your life could use a rethink.

If you have Mercury retrograde in your chart, you're likely to think before you act. You may be rather introspective. You may be a very good writer, or contrariwise, have issues to do with writing. Self-doubt can be an issue. Many of you have a very highly developed and slightly quirky sense of humour and way of communicating.

Venus retrograde

This happens once every 18 months. Venus is about love, and sometimes relationships can be a touch strained during Venus rx. It can be a time when partners feel a little more detached than usual and take time to think about how much the other person means to them. Sometimes this can bring a whole new appreciation of someone.

Venus is also about values, so during Venus rx we often re-evaluate things. It's also said that we should avoid buying big-ticket items under the Venus rx because we often change our minds later about how much we value the thing we bought!

Venus retrograde in your chart can be a blessing. You may find it easier to create abundance. Venus retrograde is also often the sign of someone who is artistic or works in the arts. In a woman's chart, it can be a symbol of trailblazing feminine expression. It can also mark shyness and insecurity.

Mars retrograde

This happens about once every two years. It can be a drag because Mars is the Go Faster planet and he likes to move forwards at all costs. And yet here we have Mars going backwards (or appearing to), which is really counter to his programming. Mars rx can be a time when we feel like we have to wade through treacle to get anywhere. However, consider the idea that there may be method in the universe's madness.

The next time Mars is going rx and you're struggling to get something down, see if perhaps you'd actually be served by slowing down a bit. One issue with Mars retrograde is that Mars is the anger planet. On the one hand, the rx can be a good time to see how your life goes if you don't lose your cool so often. On the other, it can be a time when people bottle up their anger and that's rarely a healthy thing to do.

If you have Mars retrograde on your chart, you may dislike conflict more than most. You may not be all that great at standing up for yourself. On the one hand, you don't like to start arguments and are more likely to move into peacemaker mode. On the other hand, suppressed anger is not good, so do learn to express it well.

Jupiter retrograde

The esteemed astrologer Robert Hand once said in a workshop he was giving that 'there is no such thing as a bad Jupiter transit'. And I'm pretty sure there's also no such thing as a bad Jupiter retrograde. Yes, Jupiter is the good luck planet and when Jupiter goes backwards, it might be tempting to think that somehow our luck does too. But here's another thought: what if we see Jupiter rx as a chance to have more good luck pouring down into our charts from the heavens?

For example, if Jupiter is rx in your 3rd house, you're probably going to be a tad less verbose than you usually are. You also get longer to play with the positive thinking that Jupiter brings you here. Jupiter's more thoughtful side can come out under the rx, so our Jupiter emphasis is less on wild hilarity and more on inner awareness and spiritual growth. Jupiter is rx for about six months every year.

If you have Jupiter retrograde in your chart, you may have a different set of life philosophies than most, and while you may believe in luck, and even be lucky, you're less likely to rely on that luck. Retrograde Jupiter can become an unconventional rule-breaker, whereas a direct Jupiter (i.e. not retrograde) is more law-abiding.

Saturn retrograde

Of all the retrogrades, this is one of my personal favourites. Saturn is the building planet; in fact, Saturn rules architecture and buildings themselves. So what happens if Saturn goes rx? No, everything doesn't fall down! Rather, it's time to stop trying to build things and instead, rebuild and restructure them. Another thing to consider is that Saturn is the Lord of Karma – karma can be sorted out under the Saturn rx.

Also remember that Saturn is the teaching planet and when he retrogrades, he spends a lot more time in one part of your chart. So ask yourself what lessons you're learning from his longer-than-expected stay in whichever house his rx falls. Along the same lines, note that the Saturn rx cycle is also a very good time to work on virtues such as patience, self-discipline and self-restraint. Try harder! Saturn retrogrades for about 4.5 months a year.

If you have Saturn retrograde in your chart, you may internalize your fears, which is not a good thing to do. Learn to talk about them! You may have a dislike for authority, or situations in which you need to be on your best behaviour.

Uranus retrograde

Consider this: the planet of chaos and All Things Unpredictable is storming through your chart, causing mayhem and curve balls. When Uranus rx-es, the forwards motion of the chaos stops for a moment. Which is not to say that it stops altogether, it just stops blazing a trail through your chart, hitting planets and moving through houses. To be fair, Uranus is quite a slow-moving planet, but the fact is, he does stop moving forwards with his chaos at the time of the rx.

Does he go backwards and redo some of the chaos he caused earlier, as he retraces his steps? Yes, but there are lessons on this. Keep reading and you'll learn about the beauty of three-pass retrogrades. Uranus is retrograde for around half the year.

If you have Uranus retrograde in your chart, you may be uncomfortable with change. You may wish to be rebellious but hold back.

Neptune retrograde

Neptune is always so hard to write about because it's the misty planet of weirdness and deception! What you need to know is that Neptune is rx for about five months every year. Neptune is about dreams and visions and when he's going backwards, his sensitivity is heightened.

Neptune can also be about confusion, so if you have Neptune afflicting one of your planets (i.e. squaring or opposing one of your planets or even conjoining it), you will feel more confusion for longer. Sometimes there are things we don't want to admit to ourselves, and the Neptune rx can pull the wool from our eyes so we decide to no longer kid ourselves. We realize we've been wearing rose-coloured glasses.

If you have Neptune retrograde in your chart, you may be uncomfortable with spiritual matters; or contrariwise, you may think long and hard about spiritual life.

Pluto retrograde

Pluto is retrograde for about 160 days a year, in one block. These are really important times for us all, if the Pluto rx is affecting our chart strongly (i.e. aspecting a planet or angle). Pluto's effects are usually psychological rather than tangible. There is always some kind of tearing down.

When Pluto is going backwards and then forwards and then backwards again, it's like a shredding as something in our lives gets torn down, then torn down again and torn down yet again for good measure. That might sound really intense, and it can be; however, Pluto is the planet of rebirth, so once the cycle is over and you see what you're left with after the Plutonic storm, you may even find that you've somehow either shed your skin like a snake or had some kind of total rebirth.

If you have Pluto retrograde in your chart, you may feel as though you can't unleash your powers on the world. You may fear being controlled.

A thought about the Sun and Moon

Remember, the Sun and Moon don't retrograde. Since the Earth travels around the Sun and the Moon around the Earth, the optical illusion described above isn't possible. Consider the fact that the Sun and Moon rule Leo and Cancer respectively. What do you think having a guiding luminary that never reverses means for those signs? What might it mean for the houses in your chart that have Cancer and Leo on their cusp? For one thing, you move forwards in the matters that pertain to those houses, quite relentlessly, rarely pausing.

The three passes of a retrograde

To recap, when a planet retrogrades, it starts to look like it's going backwards. In other words, it starts to retrace its steps. So now let's imagine Pluto is rx and that he just went over your Sun. As the rx starts, Pluto starts to go backwards – to where he has just been. In other words, he'll reverse right back over your Sun, so you have Pluto on your Sun again. So just when you thought you'd dealt with Pluto, here he is again.

Note that this can also apply if you have Pluto or any other planet opposite or sextile or trine or square your Sun or any other planet. The point is that when a planet retrogrades, any contacts it just made with your chart get repeated and then repeated again. Read on...

So now you've had two Pluto passes to your Sun. There was the first one when Pluto was going forwards and went over your Sun; the second one when Pluto retrograded or reversed over your Sun; and then at the end of the rx what happens? Pluto changes direction and starts to move forwards again. So once more he goes over your Sun.

These are the three passes of a retrograde. Something happens in the forwards motion, then the retrograde cycle happens and we get another taste of it. And then the forwards motion begins and we get one more serving.

This can potentially happen every time a planet retrogrades, assuming it's doing so either in the same place as, or making an aspect to, one of your planets. There's a reason why this happens and if you would like to live consciously, you can work with this reason. It's my belief that a retrograde is sent when we have something we have to learn but it will take some time to inculcate. So we get the lessons once, twice, thrice!

In the case of a tricky retrograde (in other words, when it's a 'tough' planet such as Mars or Saturn making a challenging aspect such as a square to one of our planets), the aim is that the first time the retrograde hits, we learn something, we have to deal with it and we process it. One the second occasion, again we're aware of it, but hopefully it's less of a major curve ball because we now know how to handle the energies/have learned the inherent lessons. And then, on the third time it passes, we (ideally) barely even feel it, so skilled have we become at handling whatever lesson the retrograde is teaching us.

It's like the analogy of learning to drive. When you're a newborn baby, you don't know that you can't drive; you are unconsciously unskilled – i.e. you don't know that you don't know. Then, at a certain point, you learn that you can't drive; you're consciously unskilled – you know that you don't know. Then finally, you learn to drive. But at first it's a challenge – you manage it but you have to think about what you're doing: when to brake, when to accelerate and so on. You are consciously skilled. Finally, driving becomes second nature and you don't need to think about it – you are unconsciously skilled.

With a three passes retrograde, during the first rx, you might be a bit clueless about the matter that's about to be brought to your attention. Then you feel the rx and you're really aware of it. By the time the third pass/the moving forwards again covering old ground happens, you've learned how to deal with the issues. You are consciously skilled about whatever issue the retrograde has brought up.

So if and when you experience three passes in a retrograde, work consciously with the energies. Think about what the energies in your chart are all about, combine them with the energies of the transiting planet and see what lessons are in there for you.

Station days

If you go on to study and read about astrology more deeply, you'll hear about 'stations'. A station is defined from the point of view of the Earth; it's the point when a planet appears to stop moving in the sky. The planet then appears to move slowly in the opposite direction; at this point the planet is considered to be stationary retrograde. Similarly, once the planet makes a station (stops) and begins to go forwards again, this is called stationary direct.

For example, Jupiter spends more than half of every year moving forwards (astrologers call that 'direct' motion), but when Jupiter slows, stops, and turns backwards or forwards, we call that a 'station'. When Jupiter is in the process of turning forwards, astrologers say that 'Jupiter is stationary and turning direct today,' or 'Jupiter is stationary direct.'

Instead of saying that, for example, Mercury is going retrograde today, we can say 'Mercury is stationing retrograde today.' And when the rx finishes and Mercury starts to move forwards again, we can say that 'Mercury is stationing direct.'

Shadow periods

You'll also hear about the 'shadow' periods of a retrograde. This is tied to the fact that a planet's rx actually covers more ground in the chart (more degrees – remember, each sign has 30 degrees) than just the ones between the official station days.

Take the Mercury retrograde cycle of April 2017, for example. On April 10, 2017, Mercury will station retrograde (i.e go retrograde) at 4 Taurus. On May 3, Mercury will station direct (i.e. the retrograde will end) at 24 Aries. So to find the start of the shadow period, we need to look at when Mercury was at 24 Aries going forwards – i.e. before the rx started. That was March 27, 2017. So the shadow of the retrograde started on March 27 and will end when Mercury gets back to 4 Taurus, where the rx ended: in this case, May 20. So the shadow period was March 27 to May 20.

Personally, I don't attach too much importance to shadow periods – the start and end of a retrograde are the most powerful; however, you may wish to work out the shadow periods as well. Many astrologers do.

Chapter 11
The Moon's nodes

Another really good point to look at on your birth chart is the Moon's nodes – these can tell you a lot about yourself, and other people. The nodes are actually used more in Eastern astrology than in the Western tradition, which is what we're concerned with in this book; however, like many people, I find them fascinating and very useful for understanding the basic chart and also for predicting. As with the planets and signs, the Moon's nodes are represented as glyphs: these are shown below; can you find them on your chart?

Node	Glyph
North Node	☊
South Node	☋

The nodes are where the Moon crosses the ecliptic: the apparent path of the Sun (from our point of view on Earth). The North Node is where the Moon crosses the ecliptic going north, and the South Node is where she crosses the ecliptic going south. The two points are always directly opposite each other, and they are nearly always retrograde.

The South Node shows what a person did in his or her past life; it shows what he or she came into the world able to do – the things in his or her life that feel easy or comfortable. So for example, if a person has the South Node in the 7th house, relationships are easy and comfortable to them.

On the exact opposite side of the chart is the North Node. This shows what someone needs to do, and where they need to go with their life in order to find satisfaction, fulfilment and happiness. You could say this node shows our life purpose. Another nice description is North Node = fame, South Node = infamy.

Working with the Moon's nodes

'Doing' the nodes on our chart can be scary. The idea with this is that we work on ourselves in order to move away from the South Node house and towards the North Node house. We achieve this by observing our own patterns of behaviour. Here's an example of how that works:

Imagine that, on their birth chart, a person has the South Node in the 7th house, aka the house of love and relationships, and the North Node in the 1st house, aka the house of self. So, using the interpretations of the nodes given above, the South Node is where that person feels comfortable – in this case, since the 7th house is all about relationships, in relationships. However, the North Node is where we need to go, so here, the person needs to stand on his or her own two feet, since the 1st house is about the Self.

So does that mean this person should remain single during this lifetime? No, but it does mean they should learn to be independent rather than co-dependent. As much as they might like to lose themselves in the comfort and ease of relationships (South Node, 7th house), happiness and fulfilment will be found in doing their own thing (North Node, 1st house).

The meaning of the Moon's nodes

Take a look now at which house the Moon's nodes are in on your chart, and then read on to find out what this means for you. Note that the following descriptions have been reproduced from my book *Moonology* (Hay House), which I humbly recommend if you're drawn to learning more about the effects of the Moon and its phases on your life.

So, when you have...

North Node in the 1st house/South Node in the 7th house
You may be obsessed with the idea of having a relationship, but in fact, standing on your own two feet will make you happier.

North Node in the 2nd house/South Node in the 8th house
All sorts of deep and dark subjects and taboo activities might be tempting you, but getting real and sorting out your finances will make you happier!

North Node in the 3rd house/South Node in the 9th house
You may enjoy the sound of your own voice and waffling, but you'll find happiness through real communication with others.

North Node in the 4th house/South Node in the 10th house

Your career may be seducing you and making you feel it's the most important thing in the world, but home and family is what will bring you happiness.

North Node in the 5th house/South Node in the 11th house

You may be obsessed with your friends, and the idea of freedom, but what will make you happy is truly expressing yourself creatively.

North Node in the 6th house/South Node in the 12th house

The thought of running away from your life might be an enjoyable daydream, but knuckling down and doing what you have to do is actually what will fulfil you.

North Node in the 7th house/South Node in the 1st house

You stand to gain a lot from being in a relationship. Yes, your buttons might get pushed but think of the opportunities for character growth!

North Node in the 8th house/South Node in the 2nd house

While you may feel compelled to worry about your finances, like a proper grown-up, good old-fashioned hot sex is what you need right now!

North Node in the 9th house/South Node in the 3rd house

Lots of light-hearted chatter and meaningless small talk

might feel like an easy option but it's the truth that will set you free.

North Node in the 10th house/South Node in the 4th house

Family first is a wonderful motto to live by, except for now, when you have cosmic encouragement to throw yourself into your career if you want fulfilment.

North Node in the 11th house/South Node in the 5th house

You know that person you're so obsessed with and want to make your lover? He or she would more than likely be better off as your friend.

North Node in the 12th house/South Node in the 6th house

Trying to keep your life working like clockwork may seem vital but what really matters is inner peace.

Part III
PUTTING IT ALL TOGETHER

Chapter 12
An introduction to chart reading

So, now that you've worked with all the basic astrological components on your chart, it's time to put everything you've learned together. By far the best way to use the information you've absorbed so far is to test it, test it, test it! as my first teacher used to say. Test your own birth chart, and also test those of your family and friends: that means looking at your chart/their chart and seeing if you can work out how all the energies in it – the planets in the signs and the houses aspecting each other – play out. So where to start?

Taking the birth chart as a whole

When you read the birth chart of a friend or a family member, *start with their Sun*. This is where a person shines from; it's their essential self, their *real* self. No matter which sign a person has on their ascendant, once you see where their Sun is, you know something about their core, about their Self. A person's Sun shows you what they are on Earth to do.

Look at which house their Sun is in – this tells you about their life mission. Then look at which sign it's in. What messages are you getting from this information? Start to put it together. The Sun is a person's yang side, the part of them that's 'out there'. For their yin side, their emotions, you need to look to the Moon.

To understand what it means to have the Sun in any of the signs, read the *Meaning of the signs* section on pages 75–93 and apply that to your own or someone else's Sun. Can you see how it comes out of you or them?

Identifying the 'big three': Sun, Moon, Rising Sign

To recap, then: the first three things to check when looking at your own or someone else's chart are:

❖ **The Sun** – look at which sign it's in and which house it's in. The Sun shows you a person's focus and is a really good anchor when you're doing a chart reading.

❖ **The Moon** – this shows what a person needs. Which sign and house is it in?

❖ **The Rising Sign (ascendant)** – this shows you the mask that a person wears, or their veneer. Which sign is it in?

Now ask yourself, for a start, how do these three go together? Which elements are they in – are you dealing with a very watery or fiery or earthy or airy person, for example? How do their Sun, Moon and Rising Sign go together? Are they all in the same element or in clashing elements?

Once you know the big three, you definitely have the lie of the land on any birth chart. At astrology conferences, astrologers (who are notoriously precious about sharing their exact time, date and place birth data – or maybe that's just me!) usually wear little name cards giving their Sun, Moon and Rising Sign. You can tell so much from just these three.

Next, you need to look at the rest of the planets in the chart: are there lots of planets in a particular house (which suggests a focus in life)? Which aspects are the planets making to each other? Are they easy or challenging (see page 149).

Synthesizing a birth chart

The fact is, we can't interpret the position of a sign, planet or house on its own – instead, the *entire* chart must be taken as a whole. The birth chart is full of pieces of information about an individual and, using a process that astrologers call 'synthesis', these elements must be must *synthesized* into a complete picture of the person. Synthesis simply means using your own brain and ideas to weave together all the elements in a chart in a way that no book or computer-generated chart could ever do.

For example, if you're reading someone's chart and you want to understand their Venus, you should look for the following basic information about that planet:

1. The house Venus is in.

2. The sign it's in.

3. Whether it's above or below the horizon (see page 111)

4. Whether it's conjunct (i.e. directly on top of another planet or angle).

5. Which aspects it's making to other planets (see page 144).

6. Which houses Venus rules in the chart (i.e the Taurus and Libra houses).

The trick is to take in all this astrological data about that person's Venus and rattle it around in your brain until you get it as a synthesized whole and becomes, for example: 'Venus in Capricorn in the 3rd house sextile Mars (in Pisces in the 5th house), with Venus therefore ruling houses 7 and 12.'

After this, you need to ask yourself the following:

❖ What does Venus in Capricorn mean?

❖ What does Venus in the 3rd house mean?

❖ What can be expected if this Venus in Capricorn in the 3rd house is sextiling Mars?

❖ If this Venus in Capricorn sextile Mars rules houses 7 and 12, what does that say about houses 7 and 12?

❖ And how can I put all this together?

That's astrology!

Here's a personal example: I have Venus in Gemini in the 2nd house sextile Uranus in the 15th. So let's break that down...

Venus (abundance and love) in Gemini (writing) in the 2nd house (money) sextiling (harmonizing with) Uranus (the planet of astrology *and* digital matters) in the 5th house (creativity).

And I love to make my living from writing about astrology, a lot of which I do online.

A note about reading for friends and family

As you have seen already, there's a lot to learn with astrology. The truth is, you can maybe never learn it all. There are so many techniques to try, but even the basics contained in this book give a really good grounding. It's okay to learn as you go, as long as you don't unleash any dire or negative predictions on the people you read for along the way. Sure, there are negatives in astrology but they are not what we should focus on, and there's always a solution to be found in every chart problem. After a while, you'll start to feel this intuitively.

I don't know about you, but I'm a softy when it comes to my family. I tend not to look at their birth charts too often, as I will obsess and worry! However, if and when there are issues, being able to refer to a friend or family member's chart can be a huge bonus. This is especially useful with kids – you can help them see the lessons they are meant to be learning, from their birth chart and also by transit.

Chapter 13
Your astrological cookbook

This chapter comprises what astrologers call 'an astrological cookbook' – a brief, potted description of what happens when you put a planet in a sign or a planet in a house. It offers the most basic guideline possible – no one is *all* of the things described in the keywords and phrases in the cookbook. Rather, these are *some* of the main ways in which the planets, signs and houses are likely to express themselves – or be expressed, depending on how you want to see it.

And remember, how pure and close to the 'textbook' cookbook a planet will express itself depends on what else is happening to that planet in terms of the aspects it's making to other planets.

Reading the planets by sign and house position

Use the cookbook as a handy guide while you're getting started on your astrological journey. Once you really start to feel and remember the planets, signs and houses, you'll find that you no longer need to use it.

The Sun ☉

The Sun is where a person shines from; it's their essential self, their *real* self. No matter which sign a person has on their ascendant, once you see where their Sun is, you know something about their core, about their Self. Their Sun shows you what they are on Earth to do. So, adding the ideas for the Sun to the ideas for the sign, you get the following:

The Sun through the signs

For the Sun through the signs, please refer to the *Meaning of the Signs* section on pages 75–93, which delineates all the signs and their feelings and meanings. The Sun in a sign expresses as per the descriptions offered there.

The Sun through the houses

The Sun in the 1st house – you're here to shine; to show the world who you really are. You dazzle.

The Sun in the 2nd house – you're here to think about issues to do with cash, property and possessions, and values.

The Sun in the 3rd house – you're a communicator; your life focus will be on mastering communication skills.

The Sun in the 4th house – your focus in this lifetime will be on family, your private life and what 'home' really means.

The Sun in the 5th house – you're here to create and to have fun. Make 'joyful self-expression' your life motto.

The Sun in the 6th house – you're all about service to others and doing your duty, plus health and fitness, and routines.

The Sun in the 7th house – all sorts of relationships (both personal and professional) are your focus in this lifetime.

The Sun in the 8th house – you're not afraid to face life's dark side and explore taboos. Sex and finances loom large for you.

The Sun in the 9th house – travel, study, adventure, the Great Cosmic Quest – all these are your focus in this lifetime.

The Sun in the 10th house – you'll make your mark, shine your light, achieve, lead, and stand out. You have big ambitions.

The Sun in the 11th house – your friends and the groups, networks and clubs you belong to are your focus. You're sociable.

The Sun in the 12th house – you get up to secret stuff, and are here to expand your consciousness. You're sensitive and have longings.

The Moon ☽

This indicates a person's needs. They need whatever is expressed by their Moon's sign and house to get by. The sign their Moon is in tells you *how* they need it, and it also tells you about how they express their emotions. Or don't express their emotions. It tells you how they *deal* with their emotions. Then take a look at the house the Moon is in. This shows you *what* they need. Remember, the Moon moves through each sign in about two and a bit days, so it's a very personal placement. People born three days apart will likely have different Moon signs.

The Moon through the signs

Please note the Moon through the signs section is longer than the other planetary descriptions, a) to fulfil a promise I made in my book *Moonology* and b) because the Moon is my special/favourite subject!

The Moon in Aries

The Moon represents emotions and Aries is the sign that rushes ahead, so immediately you can start to guess at what Moon in Aries people are like. They race ahead emotionally – going at full pelt. They are also often quick to come to emotional conclusions. They need speed. They need you not to loiter – personally or professionally. Moon in Aries people are not to be trifled with if you have a great big wet and watery Water sign Moon like Cancer or Scorpio or Pisces. Aries Moon people are a little emotionally reckless at times. You need to thrive on that, rather than be terrified by it!

The Moon in Taurus

Taurus = steady, Moon = emotions. Taurus Moon people need Venusian things (because Taurus rules Venus), like love, romance and caring. Plus, they need people who are steady and reliable. They need sensual physical things, like high thread-count cotton sheets and great food. They may be good with money because they definitely want the material things money can buy, in the nicest possible way.

The Moon in Gemini

A person with Moon in Gemini needs to talk things through. They need to express, write, communicate. They need to get their message across. They are all about communication. They also want you to talk so they can fulfil their other need, to listen. They like ideas and they need ideas people around them, if possible. They also need books and magazines and communication and information delivery devices around them. They are not two-faced but they can be a tad flippant, emotionally. Somehow, to the right person, that's super-seductive and charming.

The Moon in Cancer
This is a great Moon to have, if you incarnate with it. The reason being that Cancer is the home and family sign and the Moon is the home and family planet. It's also the Goddess sign and planet. So if you have the Moon here (or any other planet), you're in touch with the Divine Feminine, whether you're in a female or a male body. Moon in Cancer people need nurturing and they need to nurture. They are often big eaters or feeders. They need security and they need you on the sofa next to them at night. Can be clingy.

The Moon in Leo
These folk just want to be adored. If you find someone you fancy with the Moon in Leo, they are actually sort of a pushover. They just need you to worship them, pure and simple. They also need to be recognized for the wonderful warm and magnanimous person they are. They need glitz and glamour and they need a bit of the spotlight to themselves, at least sometimes, particularly if their Moon is in really good 'condition' – i.e. harmoniously aspecting other planets. Moon in Leo people need attention.

The Moon in Virgo
These are the gentle folk. Remember the Moon is about what we need and our emotions, and Virgo is rather a mild-mannered energy, at least a lot of the time (not that Virgo doesn't have a kinky side – notoriously, they do!) Moon in Virgo needs good food, served in a healthy way, at a routine and regular time, from a clean kitchen to a rustic table in a tidy cottage. They need things to be in order, on point, and preferably naturally scented. Moon in Virgo people need nature and the Earth, and they need to disconnect electronically to spend time breathing fresh air.

The Moon in Libra
Earlier, I said that the reputation Libra has for being indecisive is unfair, and it is. But it must be said that when you're talking Moon in Libra, there could be a bit of emotional see-sawing. Libra Moon doesn't want to offend and needs things to be nice. Libra Moon needs art and beauty and harmony. And more than anything, it needs love and relationships. Libra Moon needs relationships. It needs them to the point that it will sometimes pretend everything is okay when it's not, to avoid rocking the boat. Because it needs that relationship and it needs it to be balanced and harmonious.

The Moon in Scorpio
This is a deep and intense one. The Moon absorbs and Scorpio is – in some ways – poison. We all have Scorpio somewhere in our chart, remember – by house cusp, planet or angle. Someone who incarnates with a Scorpio Moon has come here because they want to learn about the depths

of their emotional range. Doing that is one of the secrets embedded, or even buried, in their astrological chart. They also need to be nice, and not take their emotional pain out on others. Also, they must detox from and express any negative emotional entanglements such as jealousy and revenge.

The Moon in Sagittarius

On the one hand this placement is a real blessing: the Moon is emotions and Sagittarius is the light-hearted comedy sign. The Moon in Sadge (as it is often called) is very breezy and surely that's a good thing, because everyone wants to be light-hearted, yes? Or no. Sometimes the problem with Moon in Sadge is that it can be superficial and glides over emotional issues that would benefit from a bit more investigation. Sadge Moon people need Sagittarian things like adventure and travel and ethnic things. They need the chance to do some elegant and loquacious emoting. These people are not all that easy to pin down, but they aren't emotional wet blankets or 'cling-ons'.

The Moon in Capricorn

These people need power and may, for example, dream of creating or heading up a big organization. Or they're emotionally tough. They can feel hard done by when it comes to one parent or another. However, they are also incredibly emotionally resilient (in the long run) and they know how to control their emotions so they don't get the better of them. Moon in Capricorn people need order in the way other people need air. They need structure in their personal and professional lives. They may come across as emotionally cold (depending on what else is in their chart), but in fact they have feelings like everyone else – they're just better at keeping a straight emotional face. Remember, Capricorn is the sign associated with Saturn, the zodiac's tough rule-maker.

The Moon in Aquarius

These people tend to be able to detach emotionally, if and when they want to. Lucky them – at least they aren't ruled by their emotions. Think of Aquarius and thus Moon in Aquarius people as star men and women from another planet, time, dimension, galaxy and so on. They don't feel the way other people do. They are less obviously emotional, at the very least. They are emotionally pragmatic and probably have a love/hate relationship with technology, depending on how well they have or haven't mastered it. These people need to move forwards, can be a tad too cerebral, and are awesome because they don't dwell on things.

The Moon in Pisces

Think of a big fat romantic Full Moon shining over a secluded beach at midnight. There's your Pisces Moon. These people obviously need water. They can also have issues with substance abuse as they are yearning for the Divine and seeking rapture, which they often can't find by natural means in this modern world. They need music, and poetry often soothes them. They dream and they need to be allowed to do so. They may withdraw from time to time. Pisces Moon people love feeling all their emotions. If you don't want 'all the feels', you won't want to spend too much time with a Pisces Moon person!

The Moon through the houses

The Moon in the 1st house – wears their heart on their sleeve; happy to let their feelings show.

The Moon in the 2nd house – needs to be secure financially to be secure emotionally, or is emotional about money.

The Moon in the 3rd house – needs to feel human connection and to communicate through whatever means.

The Moon in the 4th house – needs home and family and to feel settled; not a great roamer.

The Moon in the 5th house – needs to have fun and show off a bit: show the rest of us how to live/party.

The Moon in the 6th house – someone you can rely on; someone who needs routine; level-headed.

The Moon in the 7th house – needs relationships and partnerships; wants to relate with others and needs love.

The Moon in the 8th house – quite possibly a mysterious or even dark character; emotionally complex.

The Moon in the 9th house – needs to travel and see the world; needs space; a great idea exchanger.

The Moon in the 10th house – needs a career and to be allowed to be ambitious; can crave status.

The Moon in the 11th house – needs friends and networks, and to feel that he or she is definitely not alone.

The Moon in the 12th house – can be a hider of emotions or even emotionally repressed. Needs lots of TLC.

The ascendant (Rising Sign)

Below is a reminder of the salient points of each ascendant (Rising Sign); see also the descriptions in Chapter 6. You can take it further by thinking more about the characteristics of the zodiac signs (see pages 75–93). As you know, the Rising Sign is how a person comes across, and the sign of the zodiac it's in flavours that.

Remember, the Rising Sign is based on the time, date and *place* of birth. So two people born at the exact same time but more than a few miles apart will likely have different Rising Signs. This also means all their houses will be different, thus affecting their whole chart.

Rising Sign in Aries – charges right on in: doesn't stop to think; suits anything red, from clothes to cars.

Rising Sign in Taurus – earthy, and possibly showing the shape that comes from loving food.

Rising Sign in Gemini – someone flighty or whimsical who breezes in and out of your company at parties. A talker.

Rising Sign in Cancer – a feeder/food lover; quite possibly large-chested if female; sentimental and emotional.

Rising Sign in Leo – can often be seen shaking and shimmying their tail feathers to their fans.

Rising Sign in Virgo – comes across as more timid than many but this can hide all sorts of things!

Rising Sign in Libra – exudes beauty, balance and harmony.

Rising Sign in Scorpio – secretive; may repress his or her feelings; hard to fathom; sexy.

Rising Sign in Sagittarius – likeable, funny, and good with a joke. May have a tendency to preach.

Rising Sign in Capricorn – appears grown-up and authoritative; gets taken seriously; avoids moaning.

Rising Sign in Aquarius – possibly wild-eyed; outside the norm; colourful, unusual and daring.

Rising Sign in Pisces – dreamy, romantic and spiritual, possibly enlightened; hippy and ethnic; gentle.

Mercury ☿

Mercury is the planet of the mind so the sign and house it's in affects the way you communicate. Mercury is the mind planet. It zips around the chart quite fast, spending a few weeks in each sign. Remember too that Mercury goes backwards (retrogrades) up to four times a year, so it's not that unusual to be born with Mercury retrograde in your chart. In that case, the interpretations are the same, although the energy may be less look-at-me and more turned inwards.

Mercury through the signs

Mercury in Aries – quick-thinking and quick-tempered; speaks first and engages brain later. People with Mercury in Aries tend to be fiery and easily end up in arguments.

Mercury in Taurus – can be stubborn, but mentally very stable. Can be mentally sluggish, and slow to make decisions. Tends towards the conventional; good with practical matters.

Mercury in Gemini – quick-witted and funny. Can talk till the cows come home and then some. Asks endless questions; writes long e-mails; incessant chatterers. Can be superficial when living negatively.

Mercury in Cancer – speaks kindly and softly; sentimental, sharp, emotional and often homely. Worries way too much. Fusses. Good at singing kids to sleep. Soothing.

Mercury in Leo – Mercury is the communications planet and Leo is the sign of the actor and showbiz. Here's someone who has our attention and keeps talking to retain the spotlight.

Mercury in Virgo – this Mercury has it all going on. Mercury = mind, Virgo = detail-loving to the point of pernickety-ness. Can be a tad too no-nonsense. It's not all about being smart.

Mercury in Libra – wants to think beautiful thoughts and hear and speak and write beautiful words. Amusing at parties. Slick. Very good at bringing peace and harmony where there was upset. Negotiators and charmers.

Mercury in Scorpio – wants to get to the bottom of things; needs to know; probing. Sexual mind. Strong and silent type. Loves mysteries. May wish to talk dirty; has a 'dirty' mind, in a good way.

Mercury in Sagittarius – upbeat, optimistic and ready to crack a joke and have a laugh. May become preachy. May need to pay a bit more attention. Reckless. Often needs to work on being responsible.

Mercury in Capricorn – serious-minded and with an authoritative voice that others find easy to take seriously. Loves history. Is logical. Is often all about the truth. Needs integrity.

Mercury in Aquarius – a free-thinker. Aquarius is the sign of technology. These people can think ahead of the curve. Sometimes brutishly frank, they need to work on being more sensitive.

Mercury in Pisces – visionary people who can see a very wide picture. Dreamy and poetic. Have a tendency to over-romanticize. Idealists. Film and/or music buffs. Usually have an artistic streak.

Mercury through the houses

Mercury in the 1st house – will be seen as a thinker, a talker, or other Mercury-style person. Mercury people wear their Mercury on their sleeves.

Mercury in the 2nd house – always has one eye on finances. Thinks a lot about cash, property and possessions. Knows how to make money. Mathematical mind.

Mercury in the 3rd house – this person will be a talker/thinker/writer. It's what they call a 'double whammy' – the communications planet in the communications house. Someone erudite.

Mercury in the 4th house – this person has their home and family front of mind. He or she likes to think about the past. Could be quite private, and inward-looking.

Mercury in the 5th house – the mind planet Mercury is centred on the Fun Zone of the chart. What does that tell you about this person? They're fun to be around and playful. Often self-expressive/creative.

Mercury in the 6th house – focuses a lot on work and all the duties that need doing. Thinks a lot about how best to sort out everyday life. A busy person. Interested in health and alternative remedies and therapies.

Mercury in the 7th house – will think a lot about love over the course of his or her lifetime. Life may be all about thinking about other people. Can be all about romance. Talks or writes about love.

Mercury in the 8th house – thinks a lot about sex. Or money. Or both! The mind is focused on the darker side of life, sometimes. Talks about the things others consider taboo.

Mercury in the 9th house – this is a great placement, in theory (depending on what other planets Mercury connects to in the chart). This is the mind planet in the Wide Open Zone of the chart. Travel and study loom large.

Mercury in the 10th house – the focus is on career and profession. Could be a very good strategic planner. Thinks about the consequences and makes plans. Transits to Mercury will often trigger career events.

Mercury in the 11th house – loves to be with friends. Social and connected. Likes to brings groups together or go to large events and listen. Understands the concept of the Law of Attraction and wishes.

Mercury in the 12th house – could be quite psychic. Must be encouraged not to focus on his or her fears. Someone with this placement will double-benefit from meditation. Needs time alone. Retreats work well.

Venus ♀

Since Venus relates to love and money, many students are keen to discover this quickly! The sign and house Venus is in, plus which aspects Venus makes to other planets in your chart, affect the way you love and relate, as well as how easily you can draw abundance to you. Once you know a person's Venus, you know what they love, what makes them feel loved and how to show them that you love them.

Venus through the signs

Venus in Aries – Aries is a very impetuous energy so when the romance and riches planet turns up too, you can see there's an impetuous lover around. The Venus force is strong in this one. Often very attractive.

Venus in Taurus – pheromones ahoy! Beautiful and elegant, yet earthy. Loves the sensual touch. Good in the kitchen. May be an amazing cook or chef. In males, has a good idea of what women want.

Venus in Gemini – loves words, and people who use words well. May be fickle in love. Short attention span when it comes to money; can make money through self-expression. Flirtatious.

Venus in Cancer – homely and caring and makes you feel welcome, probably with some food. Good at cuddling, and making a house feel like a home. Is very protective of his or her cubs.

Venus in Leo – wants to razzle-dazzle you and probably will, well into old age. Also wants beautiful arm candy – and beautiful everything. Venus in Leo is a princess used to the best.

Venus in Virgo – loves details. Loves to look after you and be of service. May ask rather a lot of you and criticize you (if you matter to them). Likes his or her lovers to be literally very clean, preferably smelling of soap. Can be quite kinky behind closed doors.

Venus in Libra – Venus is arguably at her best here. Sweet and gentle, and with impeccable manners. The men may kiss your hand. The main caution: they love to love and it has to be lovely love. Die-hard romantics. Good relaters.

Venus in Scorpio – now here is a dark and seductive Venus. She certainly won't reveal all of herself to you. Men and women with this placement tend towards the smouldering. May be jealous. Intense.

Venus in Sagittarius – a flighty lover who can be here today and gone tomorrow, and then back the next day. Not afraid to show you that he/she cares. Free and easy, and won't cling on (dislike clingers themselves).

Venus in Capricorn – this is a toughie because these people often fear or even feel they are not loved enough. They tend to be very straight-up lovers who won't let you down, unless they're threatened.

Venus in Aquarius – he/she is coolly seeking an unconventional lover. One of the non-clingy types. Can be too mental and not heart enough. Tends to be very elegant and fashion-forward. Has lots of friends. An idealist.

Venus in Pisces – dreamy and kind; may be a little too soft and sentimental for the modern world. Loves beauty and imagination. Affectionate, and attracts people with warmth. Wears rose-coloured glasses.

Venus through the houses

Venus in the 1st house – these people are upfront about love matters. Usually look good and have a great sense of style.

Venus in the 2nd house – these people have a strong appreciation of what really matters. Appreciate quality.

Venus in the 3rd house – they are sociable, and very good at heartfelt and pleasant-to-receive communication.

Venus in the 4th house – can make home a wonderful place to be. Devoted to the family. Cosy.

Venus in the 5th house – he or she is charming, and devil-may-care when it comes to love. Charismatic.

Venus in the 6th house – will do everything possible to make work a more beautiful place to be.

Venus in the 7th house – this person is all about love and relationships, and makes a good partner.

Venus in the 8th house – can size up people and things. Makes a deep and mysterious lover. Sexual.

Venus in 9th house – a person with a love of travel or study, or the exotic, or education or religion.

Venus in the 10th house – brings professional success. This person is popular at work and a good money-earner.

Venus in the 11th house – loves their friends and their friends love them. A sociable person. Artistic friends. Strong female network.

Venus in the 12th house – may be scared of showing feelings or even of relationships. Hides beauty and artistic talent. Secret love affairs.

Mars ♂

Mars is the planet of sex and drive and determination, and pushing to get what you want. The sign and house Mars is in affects the way we chase things in life. Mars is also the way people fight, and the kinds of thing they fight about. For example, Mars in Gemini will talk you to death! Mars in Libra doesn't want to fight but will fight for justice, and so on. Remember that Mars takes around two years to go around the skies.

Mars through the signs

Mars in Aries – goes after what he or she wants. Filled with desires. You may need to get out of the way!

Mars in Taurus – sheer will can push Mars in Taurus people to success. Practical. Highly sexed.

Mars in Gemini – fights with words; enthusiastic; needs freedom. Words are a turn-on.

Mars in Cancer – very protective of its own; strives to create a fortress. Not the easiest placement.

Mars in Leo – has high energy and vitality; quick to act; will happily go at the head of any pack/group.

Mars in Virgo – all about discipline and duty; may be physically gifted; very strategic.

Mars in Libra – may be argumentative in relationships. Would be better off pouring energies into peace.

Mars in Scorpio – can be dark. Highly sexed, and passion incarnate. Drawn to high drama and passionate situations.

Mars in Sagittarius – boundless energy and a spirit of adventure: a 'don't fence me in' person.

Mars in Capricorn – has fire in the belly. Ambitious, and must avoid a tendency towards ruthlessness.

Mars in Aquarius – can be rather jangly with nerves: needs to unplug. Dynamic. Fights for humanity.

Mars in Pisces – has lots of feelings, and is not always sure how best to expend them. Yoga/Tai chi can help.

Mars through the houses

Mars in the 1st house – can come across as direct, or even overly assertive. Needs to work through aggression.

Mars in the 2nd house – can be in a hurry to accumulate wealth and is ready to do 'what it takes' to get it.

Mars in the 3rd house – these people can hardly stop themselves from saying what they think.

Mars in the 4th house – has a drive for family, and to create a home. May need to simmer down at home.

Mars in the 5th house – a bundle of energy. Someone who wants to go out and have fun, and does so! Sporty.

Mars in the 6th house – very driven at work, and willing to work hard for others. Can be a very healthy and health-conscious person.

Mars in the 7th house – can be a provocateur; a forceful partner; needs to learn not to pick fights!

Mars in the 8th house – keen to go deeper in life. Needs to develop patience regarding sex and money.

Mars in the 9th house – can become a crusader for a belief. A motivated traveller and student.

Mars in the 10th house – determined to succeed; hungry for recognition and willing to chase after it.

Mars in the 11th house – can be aggressive with friends, or motivated to have a lot of them.

Mars in the 12th house – may repress anger. Spiritual exercises such as Tai chi are recommended.

Jupiter ♃

What about your Jupiter, the planet of good luck? Arguably, Jupiter simply amplifies the characteristics of the sign it's in. The only caution with Jupiter is excess – overdoing it – and complacency. Wherever you have Jupiter in your chart, of course, things are likely to flow more easily for you. Jupiter takes around a year to move through all the signs.

Jupiter through the signs

Jupiter in Aries – full of *joie de vivre*; excited; in the mood to have fun and party a lot of the time; wilful!

Jupiter in Taurus – can do well financially. Pleasure-loving; indulgent; jealous. Connected to the Divine Feminine.

Jupiter in Gemini – very talkative, open-minded and smart; a big flirt and a traveller. Attracts or creates change.

Jupiter in Cancer – homely and caring. Food is an adventure. Family-oriented. Sympathetic, and very emotional.

Jupiter in Leo – razzle-dazzle and showmanship. Magnanimous. Can be quite flash. Life-affirming.

Jupiter in Virgo – pays a lot of attention to detail. Critical. Terribly practical and down-to-earth; matter-of-fact.

Jupiter in Libra – elegant, artistic and sociable. Loves to love and will probably love a lot. Often popular and attractive.

Jupiter in Scorpio – sexy, unfathomable and mysterious. Has a hidden agenda and lots of secrets. Dignified.

Jupiter in Sagittarius – an adventurer, risk-taker and traveller. High-spirited and devil-may-care.

Jupiter in Capricorn – pragmatic, conscientious and functional. Self-controlled. Makes big plans; enjoys work.

Jupiter in Aquarius – owns lots of gadgets, enjoys progress and technology. Humane, and makes a contribution.

Jupiter in Pisces – lots of psychic ability/intuition. Enjoys reveries. Easy-going, and runs on feelings.

Jupiter through the houses

Jupiter in the 1st house – cheery, has a jolly disposition. Prone to weight gain. Seen to fare well in life.

Jupiter in the 2nd house – a great placement for having lots of cash, but must watch excess spending.

Jupiter in the 3rd house – a big talker; chatty. Open-minded and adventure-loving. A big reader and/or writer.

Jupiter in the 4th house – enjoys home and family life. Has very protective tendencies. Enjoys big families.

Jupiter in the 5th house – takes centre-stage. Takes big risks; gambles. Flirtatious, sexy, and sexually adventurous.

Jupiter in the 6th house – enjoys routine and timetables. Has a lively daily life. A pleasure to have as a co-worker.

Jupiter in the 7th house – has lots of partners, and possibly lots of marriages. Or lots of yearning for love.

Jupiter in the 8th house – delves into the dark side of life, the mysterious and occult. Sexual. A good placement for finances.

Jupiter in the 9th house – suits publishing, travelling, seeing the world, philosophy; this is a big-picture person.

Jupiter in the 10th house – can achieve success professionally; very good in worldly affairs; recognized or famous.

Jupiter in the 11th house – popular and has big hopes and wishes. Keen to help the world; philanthropic.

Jupiter in the 12th house – there's lots of mystery about this person. A water baby; a dreamer. Soulful and very poetic.

Saturn ♄

And what about your Saturn, the planet of hard work and fear? When you're looking at Saturn, remember that it stays in each sign for around two years, so looking at Saturn through the signs says a lot about *all* the people born within a two-year (or so) period. It will talk about how they work and their relationship with other Saturnian qualities and characteristics, such as learning and teaching and going the long haul in your relationships and commitments.

As you've learned, there are positive and negative traits with all planets, but Saturn focuses on the less light-hearted ones. Of course, not everyone will express these traits, and the aspects that the other planets are making to Saturn will affect how they play out. A Venus trine will sweeten things, for example, whereas a Mars (Fire) square would add fire to the fuel (Saturn).

Saturn through the signs

Saturn in Aries – military-like discipline, organized and determined: if these are wisely channelled, a Saturn in Aries person can be a high achiever.

Saturn in Taurus – has a fear of money; shows strength of purpose; can be hard to budge; sometimes selfish.

Saturn in Gemini – a negative thinker: may focus on fear. Has an organized mind and an authoritative tone.

Saturn in Cancer – caring (or a carer); fearful; a worrier; has a strong family life. Often a very strong character.

Saturn in Leo – the autocrat who struggles to shine his or her light. Stunted expression; hides light.

Saturn in Virgo – takes care in all matters; can be too critical; frets over the details. Needs to lighten up.

Saturn in Libra – serious, and often seriously charming. Has balanced judgement. 'Good' at long-term relationships.

Saturn in Scorpio – has deep dark secrets, and embraces the dark side. Strong willpower; a formidable opponent.

Saturn in Sagittarius – dignified; can concretize ideas; tempers fun with work; serious about religion.

Saturn in Capricorn – calculating; potential for serious professional success; a workhorse.

Saturn in Aquarius – shows common sense; works for progress; scientific; exact; good with computers.

Saturn in Pisces – can dwell on the negative; works with music, the occult or in spiritual fields; relaxed; serious.

Saturn through the houses

Saturn in the 1st house – serious, and someone that others take seriously; should avoid being dour. People see Saturn when he/she walks into a room. Should avoid taking themselves too seriously. Contrariwise, often has great comic timing.

Saturn in the 2nd house – organized with cash, and may express this as a fear of money. If so, deal with that by financially planning and strategizing long-term. It will really help. A solid saver.

Saturn in the 3rd house – a tendency to look on the negative side. Needs to train the brain to notice the positive too. Living positively, a rigorous thinker; living negatively, a rigid thinker. Serious communications.

Saturn in the 4th house – builds a very solid personal life and home base. Family issues are possible. Needs to sort out private life dramas by being mature and smart. Has karmic relationships with family members, with lots of 'past life' issues to resolve.

Saturn in the 5th house – needs to schedule in fun, or they might forget to let their hair down. Lessons in life come from romance and kids. Seriously creative. Needs to avoid being a killjoy; and needs to express themselves.

Saturn in the 6th house – a great place to have Saturn. Good at living in rhythm, with routines and timetables; a conscientious and helpful worker. The workaday planet in the workaday house. But don't work too hard!

Saturn in the 7th house – learns the most important life lessons via relationships: the 'true' lover. Needs to love more lightly! This can be a tricky placement if lovers are not chosen wisely. Otherwise, great for relationship longevity.

Saturn in the 8th house – good at making long-term money plans. Needs to choose financial partners wisely! With good choices, solid finances beckon. Poor choices could lead to hardship. Needs to work through fears.

Saturn in the 9th house – this person loves to study, and is serious about knowledge; good for working in publishing, travel or education. May need help to see the bigger picture. Travels for work. Honourable.

Saturn in the 10th house – seriously ambitious and works like a dog: fears professional failure. This is a make-or-break placement. There are not many corners to be cut. Authoritarian, and likes to instruct.

Saturn in the 11th house – important life lessons from friends; needs to work on believing that he or she is loved by pals. Humane. Choosy about who he/she befriends, and thus has enduring friendships.

Saturn in the 12th house – may be reclusive; potentially very spiritual, and disciplined about carrying out spiritual practices. Expressed negatively, can breed sorrows. Daily meditation will really help.

Uranus ♅

And what about the maverick planet of chaos, Uranus? Uranus takes around 84 years to go around the zodiac, which means it stays in each sign for about seven years. Wherever Uranus goes, disruption and progress follow. Because Uranus stays in each sign for such a long time, lots of people born within a seven-year range will have Uranus in the same sign. Thus, whole clusters of people seek to do the Uranian thing and upturn convention and move things forwards.

Therefore, we say that Uranus is generational, in that it affects large numbers of people in the same ways. For example, most people born between 1968 and 1975 have

Uranus (change) in Libra (relationships). In the West, this is the generation that moved relationships forwards to the existing, more modern set-up. Note also that Uranus is the planet of liberation and Libra is the sign ruled by Venus, the planet of the feminine, and we had women's liberation during this time. Uranus is shocking – think of how shocked polite society was when women started metaphorically burning their bras.

For another example, most people born between 1988 and 1995 have Uranus in Capricorn. These are the people who will stir up and create changes to (Uranus) business and society's working business models (Capricorn). Online (Uranus) enterprises (Capricorn) are revolutionizing (Uranus) business (Capricorn).

Visit theastrologybook.com/Uranus for a list of when Uranus went in and out of the signs in the last 100 or so years.

Uranus through the signs

Uranus in Aries – rebellious, impossible to tether, and doesn't mind at all who knows it. A bit wild.

Uranus in Taurus – surprisingly romantic and romantically surprising; needs to avoid selfishness and stubbornness.

Uranus in Gemini – free-thinking; modern ideas; chaotic communications; original ways of thinking; inventive.

Uranus in Cancer – may have a rather chaotic home/family life, or be part of a very modern family; unconventional lifestyles; eccentric.

Uranus in Leo – rebels; can be a bit hysterical. These people are game-changers, creatives, and love to move forwards. Unique self-expression.

Uranus in Virgo – progress in alternative health/vibrational medicine; changes to feminine status quo; clever.

Uranus in Libra – changes to the way we 'do' relationships; maverick romantics; different partnership norms.

Uranus in Scorpio – sexually progressive; upturns fixed ideas; needs to avoid vengefulness, often has highly charged emotions.

Uranus in Sagittarius – no-holds-barred; progress at all costs; reckless; unorthodox; nervous.

Uranus in Capricorn – unconventional in career matters; restless; professional one-offs; innovative.

Uranus in Aquarius – scientific; humane; dragging the world into the future; digital talents; inventions; freedom.

Uranus in Pisces – idealism; new ideas related to mysticism; modernization of music and art; changeable.

Uranus through the houses

Uranus in the 1st house – someone who comes across as different: a maverick, liberated, does their own thing.

Uranus in the 2nd house – changeable finances; unusual ways to make money; works well solo; changing values.

Uranus in the 3rd house – a true freethinker; lives outside the box; original; mentally undisciplined; genius.

Uranus in the 4th house – unconventional family life with many different homes; technology at home; leaves roots.

Uranus in the 5th house – chaotic love life; free-love free-sex attitudes; untethered creativity; digital talents.

Uranus in the 6th house – works digitally; self-employed; unusual working life; chaotic routines; daily changes.

Uranus in the 7th house – unusual partners; commitment issues; marital freedom; unconventional, romantically.

Uranus in the 8th house – sexually explorative and non-traditional; roller-coaster finances; may bring unexpected legacies.

Uranus in the 9th house – a rebellious mind; a seeker of cosmic truths; unusual travel and study; erratic education.

Uranus in the 10th house – a professional maverick; changes jobs; works well solo/digitally; unpredictable work.

Uranus in the 11th house – changes groups of friends; drawn to unusual people; wishes for unusual things.

Uranus in the 12th house – has visions of the future; hides peccadillos; may feel very different to other people.

Neptune ♆

Now we come to the planet of dreams and soulmates. Again this is a very slow-moving planet and therefore is considered 'generational' (see page 47). Neptune takes about 165 years to go through all 12 signs, staying in each one for approximately 14 years. Note that the downside of Neptune is confusion and disappointment. So wherever Neptune is found in your chart, or goes by transit, disappointment or confusion can follow.

However, Neptune is also about idealism, inspiration and connection to the Divine. As per my stated purpose to uplift people via astrology, I've mainly focused on those positive qualities for Neptune in the descriptions below. But if you want to apply the ideas of deception, disappointment, confusion and sacrifice to the sign or house where Neptune is, go right ahead. Both are possible, neither is obligatory.

Note that since 1900, Neptune has only been in Gemini, Cancer, Leo, Virgo, Libra, Scorpio, Sagittarius, Capricorn, Aquarius and Pisces. However, descriptions for all the sign placements are given below.

Neptune through the signs

Neptune in Aries – a great drive to discover the secrets of the unknown; subversive; idealistic.

Neptune in Taurus – musical, loving and artistic; visionary; charming; makes money through art or spirituality.

Neptune in Gemini – the daydreamer. Fanciful – a writer of fantasies; has a great imagination; a worrier.

Neptune in Cancer – dreamy: with a dream home and a dream family; appealing; emotional; lazy; very sympathetic.

Neptune in Leo – show-business and smoke and mirrors; has possibly unrealistic ideas of their own fabulousness; creative.

Neptune in Virgo – confused; critical; not sure of what it really wants; idealist about health and service.

Neptune in Libra – dreams up things of beauty, art, fashion; may experience legal confusion; romantic, visionary; a dream lover.

Neptune in Scorpio – sexual fantasies; may be sexually duplicitous; secretive; sarcastic; attracted to the occult.

Neptune in Sagittarius – dreams of travel; idealistic; seeks to merge with life through travel and study; utopian.

Neptune in Capricorn – calculating; inspires business ideas; dissolves old ways of working; a professional idealist.

Neptune in Aquarius – a desire to help humanity; charitable; digital connections; dreams of freedom.

Neptune in Pisces – spiritual awakening; gentle; no boundaries; immersed in dreams; romantic to a fault.

Neptune through the houses

Neptune in the 1st house – comes across as dreamy and romantic, possible confused; an idealist.

Neptune in the 2nd house – confusion regarding cash; needs to earn money in an inspiring way; values dreams.

Neptune in the 3rd house – ideas that uplift and inspire; intuitive; visionary; easily confused.

Neptune in the 4th house – ideal family life; uplifted by home life; inspired by family values; lives by the sea.

Neptune in the 5th house – loves to lose self while having fun, including via drugs and alcohol; a dreamy flirt.

Neptune in the 6th house – dreams of being of service; finds routines hard; works with life's mysteries.

Neptune in the 7th house – seeks and often finds a soulmate; may be inspired by a partner.

Neptune in the 8th house – tantric sex and Divine sexual union; financial rewards for performing uplifting work.

Neptune in the 9th house – a great mind that can see far and wide; has visions; understands mysteries; a seeker.

Neptune in the 10th house – career confusion possible; inspirational work leads to success and career dreams.

Neptune in the 11th house – inspires friends and finds inspiring friends; a social idealist and a humanitarian dreamer.

Neptune in the 12th house – great connection to the cosmos; uncertain fears; psychic ability; deep meditations

Pluto ♀ ♇

And finally we have the planet of power and passion. Pluto takes approximately 248 years to go through all 12 signs, staying in each sign for between 14 and 30 years. The keywords for Pluto are magic, passion, power, breaking things down, transformation, death, rebirth and taboos. Note that because Pluto is so slow, there are quite a few signs that Pluto hasn't been in recently. For example, Pluto was last in Aries between 1822 and 1853 and won't return until 2068. Even so, all the Pluto qualities you can expect to find are listed here, as are the last and most recent dates that the planet was in each sign, or the most recent and next dates.

The descriptions here are a mix between what we saw as a result of the transit of Pluto through the various signs and what we can expect from the children born when Pluto was in the different signs.

Pluto through the signs

Pluto in Aries (1822–1853; 2068–2098): brash, and determined to get ahead. Full firepower. Not afraid to change the way things are done.

Pluto in Taurus (1853–1884; 2098–2129): changing the way the world economy works; makes changes slowly but surely.

Pluto in Gemini (1882–1914; 2132–2159): blasts away old ways of thinking; revolutionary; ideas; communications.

Pluto in Cancer (1914–1937): transforms the ideal of the family unit, ideal home, ideal country, ideal ethnicity; powerful emotions.

Pluto in Leo (1937–1956): the 'baby boomers'. Powerful leaders who transformed pleasure and entertainment; a confident generation.

Pluto in Virgo (1956–1971): the people who changed the idea of duty and service and transformed alternative health.

Pluto in Libra (1971–1982): Generation X. Transforming relationships and our ideas about art; obsessed with appearances.

Pluto in Scorpio (1982–1995): deep transformation to the areas of sex, death and all things taboo. Genetic engineering. Dark.

Pluto in Sagittarius (1746–1762; 1995–2008): changing the way we are educated; social media; changes to the internet; spirituality vs religion; truth is all.

Pluto in Capricorn (1762–1778; 2008–2024): trimming the fat from business; transforming corporations; undermining governments.

Pluto in Aquarius (1778–1798; 2024–2044): transforming the way we belong to networks, and our relationship with technology; humanitarian matters.

Pluto in Pisces (1797–1823; 2044–2068) – profound changes in our connection to the Divine and our psychic abilities; opening up new channels.

Pluto through the houses

Pluto in the 1st house – can come across as powerful and passionate, or rather controlling and manipulative.

Pluto in the 2nd house – a passion for wealth that will materialize if Pluto is in good condition; values depth.

Pluto in the 3rd house – a powerful communicator who breaks down barriers and leads to new thinking; a magical person.

Pluto in the 4th house – life at home can be explosive; family will change this person's life; inner tension.

Pluto in the 5th house – intense love life; obsessions; children will change this person's life; profound creativity.

Pluto in the 6th house – intense daily life; highly absorbing work; deep need to be of service; a healer.

Pluto in the 7th house – a passionate lover who must avoid controlling partners or attempting to control partners.

Pluto in the 8th house – a yearning to explore the darker, deeper realms of life; passionate sex and changing finances.

Pluto in the 9th house – seeks cosmic knowledge and to expand own horizons and knowledge base; metaphysical.

Pluto in the 10th house – desire to succeed/leave a mark; a powerful professional player; a conflict with authority.

Pluto in the 11th house – has powerful friends, hidden alliances, intense friendships; a powerful manifestor and a leader.

Pluto in the 12th house – needs time alone; a magician; powerful dreams; karmic life; breaks down fears.

Chapter 14

Love, money and other secrets in your chart

Now that you have a good working knowledge of all the essential elements of your birth chart – the signs, planets, houses, aspects and so on – you can start to play around with them. So far, we've looked at everything in a relatively conventional order, but let's mix things up a little, and explore the key personal topics a birth chart reading can reveal.

Money

Would you like to know how you (or someone else) operate when it comes to money? Then you need to start with the 2nd and 8th houses: the birth chart's 'money boxes'. The 2nd house is more about your own cash, property and possessions, while the 8th house is about joint ventures and places where your money meets someone else's.

Look at the signs on the 2nd and 8th house cusps – there's a lot to learn from these! In which element are they: go get 'em Fire, practical Earth, intellectual Air or an emotional

Water sign? The signs there will indicate how a person lives out their life financially.

Next, take a look at the planets that rule those signs on the cusps. For example, if you have Scorpio ruling the 2nd house, take a look at Pluto. Where is it, and what condition is it in? What do you pick up from that? Someone who is controlling with money, perhaps? What else?

Then take a look at which planet(s) are in the 2nd and 8th houses. What sort of condition are they in? What links, or aspects, are those planets making to other planets? If one is clashing with Saturn for example (i.e. making a square or an opposition or even a conjunction), there could be fears around cash – Saturn being fear and the 2nd house being cash. But don't stop there in your interpretation. How else could restrictions around cash play out for someone?

Learning all that you can about the signs on the 2nd and 8th houses, the planet(s) in those houses and the planets that rule those houses will be very informative. Are the signs on the 2nd and 8th houses confident Fire signs? Emotional Water signs? (A Fire sign will chase cash while a Water sign is more likely to somehow 'attract' it.)

You also need to look at Venus when you're thinking about cash. Where is Venus and which aspects is she making to other planets? While you're at it, look at the 10th house as well. It's the house of ambition – how ambitious are you, or the person whose chart you're looking at? That will make a difference to your cashflow, right? As will the 6th house indications, since the 6th house is where we perform our daily duties.

Finally, you can check the 3rd house (Mind Zone) to see your own/the person's attitudes to life (some mindsets are more lucrative than others!) And also check Jupiter, which is about generosity and luck. The more generous we are, the more abundance flows.

Moreover, Mercury is about cold hard cash and Venus is about how much luxury you allow in your life. So also take a look at Mercury. What condition is it in? Is it making easy aspects to other planets? Challenging ones? This also tells you about a person's financial life.

Take it back to your birth chart

Look at your 10th house.

What sign is on the cusp and which planets are in the 10th house? Can you see how that plays out in your life? Now try the same with a friend's chart.

Love

If you want to find out about the love in your own or someone else's chart, there are several places to look. Firstly, the 2nd house is informative because it shows a person's self-esteem and that will strongly influence how they are in relationships. The Rising Sign will show you how they come across, which will give an indication of how they are in love.

The 7th house is even more important as it's effectively the Love Zone. What's going on in there, and which sign is on the cusp? And looking at that sign, how is the planet that rules it faring in the chart? What condition is it in – i.e. what aspects is it making to other planets? Is it harmonizing with an easier planet (i.e. the Sun, Moon, Mercury or Venus) or is it clashing with a harder planet such as Mars or Saturn?

What about your/their Moon? What do you/they need in a relationship? And the 5th house? That's where we flirt from, after all. Lastly, look at Venus – that tells you about love. If you're a woman it's about your femininity and also about how you'll love; if you're a man it's about the women you're likely to fall in love with. For both sexes, it's also about abundance – how you can get it, for example.

Try the following love-themed exercises:

❖ Cast a chart for your partner, potential partner or your ex's Venus and Mars. That will tell you all about them when it comes to love and sex. Can you see how true to type they are?

❖ Look at your lover or ex's descendant (aka their Love Line). That's the gateway to their love life – the sign that's on their 7th house cusp tells you a lot about how and who they love.

❖ Look at your own Mercury for how you communicate (communication being essential to good relationships), your Moon for what you need, your Venus for love, and Mars for sex. What do you see?

A quick compatibility guide

When it comes to compatibility between signs, there's a general rule of thumb: Fire and Air signs go well together, and Earth and Water go well together. However, I need to remind you that you're more than just your Sun sign. For example, a Cancerian with Venus and Mars in Gemini would get on way better with, say, Aries and Aquarius people than you might otherwise expect if you only knew their Sun sign.

The table below shows which signs get on well and which signs clash.

	Fire	Earth	Air	Water
Fire	A heavenly match!	Not so much...	A heavenly match!	Not so much...
Earth	Not so much...	A heavenly match!	Not so much...	A heavenly match!
Air	A heavenly match!	Not so much...	A heavenly match!	Not so much...
Water	Not so much...	A heavenly match!	Not so much...	A heavenly match!

Career, success and fame

This is a bit different to looking at cash. First of all, you need to look at which sign rules your Career Zone, aka your 10th house. What does that tell you about yourself, or the person whose chart you're looking at? Where is the Sun? Is it high up in the chart and showing off or buried in the 12th house, where it wants to be alone, preferably with no one looking at it?

What about the Moon? Do you crave recognition? A Moon on the *Medium Coeli* (MC) is said to indicate fame, because one of the other things the Moon represents is the general public. You can look at Jupiter to get a sense of whether you, or the person whose chart you're reading, are likely to have a public life. If it's prominent in the chart – i.e. in the 1st house – chances are you/they will impose your/their personality far and wide! But also look at drearier work planet Saturn and the 10th house to see how hard a worker someone is. That's also going to influence how well they do in life, and materially.

Take it back to your birth chart

Take a look at the sign on your 10th house.

What do you see? Ambitious Capricorn? Harmony-loving Libra? Communicative Gemini? The sign will speak of how you approach your career. Where is your Mars? How determined are you to succeed? What about Saturn? Saturn is about hard work and we all know hard work leads to success. And what about Jupiter? How does luck come into your success?

Lessons and luck

For life lessons and the luck in a chart, look at Saturn and Jupiter respectively. Wherever Saturn is in a chart, we have the most lessons to learn. Wherever Jupiter is in a chart, we have luck on our side. If these two planets join up harmoniously (with a conjunction, trine or sextile), hard work can lead to apparent good luck. If they clash (square or opposition), hard work could be the price to pay for freedom.

Riff on some Jupiter and Saturn words and see what you come up with. Saturn words are things like tough and hard and challenging, whereas Jupiter is fun and optimistic and cheerful. And where Jupiter is now is where you're extra lucky. Where Saturn is now in your chart is where you have challenges and lessons coming.

Take it back to your birth chart

Look at where Jupiter and Saturn are on your chart.

Can you see that you have more ease where Jupiter is, and more lessons where Saturn is?

Travel and adventure

For this, you need to look at the 9th house and Jupiter and see what's going on. Which sign is on the 9th house and what kind of state is the ruling planet in – i.e. what aspects is it making to other planets? Is it harmonizing or clashing with them? What about the 3rd house, aka the Mind Zone? Are you open-minded and ready to go off and see the world? What scares us can hold us back – see where Saturn is.

Take it back to your birth chart

Look at your 9th house.

Do you have the 9th house of someone who is all about adventure (for example, you may have your Sun or Jupiter in there or Sagittarius on the cusp)?

The way you come across to others

For this, you need to look at the Rising Sign, which is a subtle form of communication, the 3rd house, which is the Communications Zone, and also Mercury. Which planets are in the 3rd house, or rule it, and what condition are they in? Is Mercury making harmonious aspects to other planets or clashing with Mars, Saturn or any of the other outer planets?

If you want to get a glimpse of your level of compatibility with someone, it's worth checking to see how well your Mercury matches theirs – in other words, do you have Mercury in complementary elements? Physical attraction is a big thing but so is mental connection! Or maybe your Mercury harmonizes your partner's Venus or Jupiter, so there is good feeling between you when you communicate.

Take it back to your birth chart

Look at your Rising Sign, 3rd house and Mercury.

Can you see how these three express the way you come across and communicate with others?

Family life

This is found in the 4th house and the Moon. Which sign is on the 4th house cusp and in what condition is that sign's planet? In other words, is that planet harmonizing with other planets or clashing with them? Which sign is on the 4th house and what condition is the ruling planet in? Is it harmonizing or clashing with other planets? To find that out, check to see what aspects the planet ruling that house is making to other planets. What about planets *in* the 4th house? What condition are they in?

Take it back to your birth chart

Look at the sign on your 4th house.

Next, look at the planet that rules that sign. Where is that planet and what condition is it in? Can you see how all this describes your home life?

Children

For this, check out the 5th house. (Grandchildren are the 10th house.) Which sign is on the 5th house cusp, and what condition is that sign's planet in – i.e. what aspects is it making to other planets? Harmonious or clashing? What about the planets in the 5th house? What condition are they in?

Take it back to your birth chart

Look at the planets in your 5th house.

These will go some of the way to describing your kids. For your grandkids, look to the 10th House (that's because they are your kids' kids: the 5th house after the 5th house. Get it?)

Health

Check out the 6th house for the main health headlines. Also look at Mars. For example, are you or the person whose chart you're reading ever going to exercise? Obviously someone with a good relationship with exercise has a better chance of good health! Check the Sun for vitality. Is it harmonizing with Mars or being pressured by Saturn, for example.

Is Saturn on the 6th house cusp, or in the 6th house or conjunct with Mars? This can block the flow of good energies. However, remember that Saturn loves discipline so it can also be good for getting into good exercise routines and regimes. Look at the Moon, too – what do you need and are you getting it?

Take it back to your birth chart

Use your Mars as a health indicator.

Where is your Mars, and which sign is it in? Is it harmonizing with other planets or clashing with them? This will tell you a lot about your relationship with exercise!

Sex

To know more about someone's sex life (or your own) look to the 5th house, 8th house and Mars. Look at those houses' rulers. Which sign and what kind of condition are they in? Are they harmonizing with other planets or clashing? What about planets in the 5th house? What condition are they in? That will tell you a lot about a person's sex life and their attitudes to sex.

Take it back to your birth chart

Look at your 8th house.

Which sign rules it? What does that say about your attitude to and experience of sex? Also look at your Mars – the sign and house it's in. What does it tell you?

Creativity

Creativity is found in the 5th house. So take a look at the sign on the 5th house and also at any planets in there. Also look at the ruler of your 5th house (i.e. the planet that rules the sign that's on the house). Venus and Neptune both also have a creative vibe. See what's going on with Venus for a sense of your own/someone else's creativity.

Take it back to your birth chart

Look at your 5th house.

This house shows you how you like to have fun and express yourself. What do you see in there? If there are no planets in your 5th house, which sign is on the 5th house cusp and which planet rules that sign? What does it tell you?

Fears

Look to Saturn and the 12th house for these. The sign on the 12th house cusp and the planet that rules that sign will tell you a lot about what you/someone else fears. Look also to Saturn in your/their chart. The house that Saturn is in will also tell you about what worries you/them (but equally about where the important lessons lie, since Saturn is all about lessons).

Take it back to your birth chart

Find your Saturn.

Wherever you have Saturn in your chart, you can find fears that you have to get over. Which house is Saturn in and which aspects is it making to other planets in your chart? That will tell you a lot about your fears. Time to work on them!

Making friends

What about how you function in a group? Look at the sign on your 11th house. Now look at the planet ruling that sign. What condition is it in? Is it harmonizing or clashing with other planets? Are there planets in your 11th house? What are they up to? Are they harmonizing or clashing with other planets?

Take it back to your birth chart

Look at your Mercury and Venus.

These planets will also tell you about what you're like as a friend – how you communicate and who you love. Take a look at them now, assess their condition and see how that plays out in your life.

Life purpose

For this, you need to look to the karmic Moon's nodes. The South Node is what you came into this life with. The North Node is where happiness and fulfilment live, waiting for you to find it and do it! For a fuller explanation of the nodes, see Chapter 11.

Chapter 15
Predictive astrology

Although this book's focus is natal astrology, predictive astrology is such a wonderful and fun part of astrology, I'd like to offer a short guide to making predictions. Here's the idea behind it...

What are predictions?

As you know, the planets move around the Sun, and your birth chart is a map of where the planets were when you were born, set for the place you were born. But of course, the planets didn't stop moving around the Sun after you were delivered; rather, they kept on moving and they are still moving!

In Chapter 8 you learned about the degrees. These are the actual spots within the 30-degree measurement of the zodiac signs where the planets in your birth chart can be found. By the same token, the planets up in the skies (called 'transiting' planets) are all still moving through the imaginary degrees astrologers apply to the zodiac.

In that same chapter you also learned that planets make aspects (angles) to each other in your birth chart – that's when we can measure them to be, say, 30 or 90 or 120 degrees apart (a sextile, a square and a trine).

Now consider the idea that the planets in the sky can make aspects or angles to the planets in your birth chart. So, let's say that Saturn in the skies (aka transiting Saturn) is at 10 degrees of Sagittarius and the Sun in your birth chart is at 10 degrees of Aquarius. We would say that transiting Saturn is sextiling your natal Sun.

Now we can start to make predictions. We know that Saturn is very constructive and helps us to build our lives. This is especially the case when the planet is in a positive frame of mind – i.e. when it's making a harmonious or easy aspect (in this case, a sextile) to your Sun, which is the essential you. Thus when Saturn sextiles your Sun, it's a good time for you to grow as a person, to mature, to do Saturnian things like make commitments and plan out some proper life strategies.

Do you see what I did there? I applied information about the planets and signs and then added the backdrop of the houses. So for example, if transiting Saturn is in your 3rd house, then 3rd house issues apply. Therefore it's a good time to think through and seriously (Saturn) discuss (3rd house) these issues.

A note about the Astrological Cookbook

The interpretations in the Astrological Cookbook (Chapter 13) were written mainly with the individual's chart in mind. However, the meaning for each planet in each sign and house can also be extrapolated to extract its meaning when it's a transit. So you can start to use the information in the cookbook section to help you make predictions.

For example, if you were born with your Sun in the 1st house, you were born to shine. However, when the transiting Sun is in your 1st house, it's also your time to shine... get it? The planets in your birth chart and the planets transiting and making angles to your birth chart all carry the same or extremely similar meanings. Mercury is always about communication – in your chart or in the skies/transiting; Venus is always about love, Mars is always about being determined, and so on.

Making predictions with an ephemeris

In order to start making predictions, you'll need to get hold of an ephemeris: a book showing where the planets are at any given time. They are available online, or you can buy software that provides the same information (I use Solar Fire, which I consider the best). For a great online ephemeris, see khaldea.com/ephemcenter.shtml

On the following page is an example of an ephemeris: it might look complicated, but in fact it's not hard to read once you get to grips with the array of little numbers it contains.

On this ephemeris, you can see the dates in January 2016 on the far left column. Along the top you see all the glyphs for the planets. In the second column is sidereal time – this is the time worked out from the motion of the Earth relative to the stars rather than relative to the Sun.

Then, under the planetary glyphs, you see the degrees and minutes for where each planet is. If you look down the column, you'll see that there are numbers, numbers, numbers and every now and then, a zodiac sign glyph. The signs show when the planet changes signs. So for example

KHALDEA Ephemeris				JANUARY 2016				Geocentric Longitudes - 0.00 GMT					
	☉	☽	☿	♀	♂	♃	♄	♅	♆	♇
1	9V358'56	26♈42'10	25♈36.1'	29♈16'58	2✗03'28	28≏33'23	23♏09'16	11✗08'33	16♈34'22	7✗32'44	15V302'54
2	11 00 05	R 31 52	25 37.9'	29 56'35	2 16'19	29 06'41	23 10'33	11 15'04	16 34'41	7 34'10	15 04'58
3	12 01 15	20 19 39	25 29.7'	0♉27'43	3 29'14	29 39'54	23 11'39	11 21'32	16 35'04	7 35'37	15 07'02
4	13 02 24	2♉11 05	26 26.5'	49'27	4 42'12	0♏13'03	23 12'34	11 27'58	16 35'30	7 37'05	15 09'07
5	14 03 34	14 11 24	25 23.4'	1 00'56	5 55'14	0 46'06	23 13'16	11 34'22	16 35'59	7 38'36	15 11'12
6	15 04 45	26 25 07	25 20.2'	1 01'26	6 08'19	1 19'04	23 13'48	11 40'43	16 36'31	7 40'08	15 13'16
7	16 05 55	8✗55 44	25 17.0'	0 50'22	9 21'27	1 51'56	23 14'07	11 47'02	16 37'06	7 41'41	15 15'21
8	17 07 06	21 45 23	25 13.8'	0 27'28	10 34'38	2 24'42	23 14'16	11 53'18	16 37'45	7 43'17	15 17'26
9	18 08 16	4V354 33	25 10.7'	29V352'46	11 47'52	2 57'23	23 14'12	11 59'32	16 38'26	7 44'53	15 19'31
10	19 09 26	18 22 05	25 07.5'	29 06'47	13 01'08	3 29'58	23 13'57	12 05'42	16 39'11	7 46'32	15 21'35
11	20 10 36	2☓05 20	25 04.3'	28 10'28	14 14'27	4 02'27	23 13'30	12 11'50	16 39'59	7 48'11	15 23'40
12	21 11 46	16 00 39	25 01.1'	27 05'16	15 27'49	4 34'49	23 12'51	12 17'55	16 40'50	7 49'52	15 25'44
13	22 12 56	0✗04 01	25 57.9'	25 53'06	16 41'12	5 07'05	23 12'01	12 23'57	16 41'43	7 51'35	15 27'48
14	23 14 04	14 11 45	24 54.8'	24 36'13	17 54'38	5 39'15	23 10'59	12 29'56	16 42'40	7 53'19	15 29'52
15	24 15 12	28 20 53	24 51.6'	23 17'05	19 08'06	6 11'18	23 09'45	12 35'51	16 43'40	7 55'04	15 31'56
16	25 16 20	12♓29 23	24 46.4'	21 58'13	20 21'35	6 43'14	23 08'20	12 41'44	16 44'43	7 56'50	15 33'59
17	26 17 26	26 35 54	24 45.2'	20 42'00	21 35'07	7 15'04	23 06'44	12 47'33	16 45'49	7 58'38	15 36'02
18	27 18 32	10♈39 30	24 42.1'	19 30'32	22 48'41	7 46'47	23 04'56	12 53'18	16 46'58	8 00'27	15 38'05
19	28 19 37	24 39 09	24 38.9'	18 25'35	24 02'16	8 18'23	23 02'56	12 59'01	16 48'09	8 02'18	15 40'07
20	29 20 42	8♉33 25	24 35.7'	17 28'25	25 15'54	8 49'52	23 00'46	13 04'43	16 49'24	8 04'10	15 42'10
21	0☓21 45	22 20 20	24 32.5'	16 39'57	26 29'33	9 21'14	22 58'24	13 10'16	16 50'42	8 06'03	15 44'11
22	1 22 48	5♊57 25	24 29.4'	16 00'39	27 43'14	9 52'29	22 55'51	13 15'48	16 52'03	8 07'57	15 46'13
23	2 23 49	19 22 05	24 26.2'	15 30'40	28 56'57	10 23'36	22 53'07	13 21'16	16 53'26	8 09'52	15 48'13
24	3 24 50	2♋32 04	24 23.0'	15 09'55	0♏10'41	10 54'37	22 50'12	13 26'41	16 54'53	8 11'48	15 50'14
25	4 25 51	15 25 49	24 19.8'	14 58'05	1 24'27	11 25'29	22 47'06	13 32'01	16 56'22	8 13'46	15 52'13
26	5 26 50	28 02 54	24 16.6'	14 54'44	2 38'15	11 56'14	22 43'49	13 37'19	16 57'54	8 15'44	15 54'13
27	6 27 49	10♈24 08	24 13.5'	14 59'21	3 52'04	12 26'51	22 40'21	13 42'32	16 59'28	8 17'44	15 56'11
28	7 28 47	22 31 33	24 10.3'	15 11'22	5 05'55	12 57'19	22 36'42	13 47'41	17 01'06	8 19'44	15 58'09
29	8 29 44	4≏28 17	24 07.1'	15 30'14	6 19'47	13 27'40	22 32'53	13 52'46	17 02'46	8 21'45	16 00'06
30	9 30 41	16 18 26	24 03.9'	15 55'22	7 33'41	13 57'52	22 28'54	13 57'47	17 04'29	8 23'48	16 02'03
31	10 31 37	28 06 41	24 00.8'	16 26'15	8 47'37	14 27'55	22 24'44	14 02'44	17 06'14	8 25'51	16 03'59

Figure 22: Ephemeris

here, looking at the column showing the Sun's position (i.e. the column with the glyph for the Sun at the top), the Sun moves into Aquarius on 21 January.

Where are the planets right now?

To find out where the planets are right now, go to theastrologybook.com/freechart and cast a 'here and now chart' by keying in today's date, and your location. Your chart will look similar to the 'here and now' chart I've created today, as I write this book:

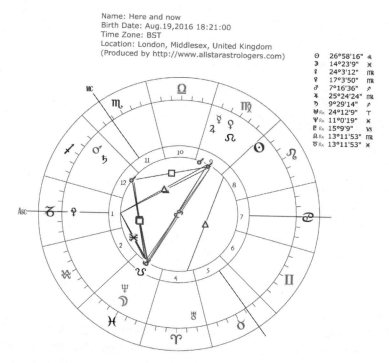

Name: Here and now
Birth Date: Aug.19,2016 18:21:00
Time Zone: BST
Location: London, Middlesex, United Kingdom
(Produced by http://www.allstarastrologers.com)

☉	26°58'16"	♌
☽	14°23'9"	♓
☿	24°3'12"	♍
♀	17°3'50"	♍
♂	7°16'36"	♐
♃	25°24'24"	♍
♄	9°29'14"	♐
♅ Rx	24°12'9"	♈
♆ Rx	11°0'19"	♓
♇ Rx	15°9'9"	♑
☊ Rx	13°11'53"	♍
☋ Rx	13°11'53"	♓

Figure 23: Here and now birth chart

On my 'here and now' chart, the Sun is in Leo, the Moon is in Pisces, Mercury is in Virgo and so on. You can see all this in the chart and it's also listed on the top right of the chart.

Now let's look at the birth chart of a woman born at 8.30 a.m. on 21 March 1966 in London:

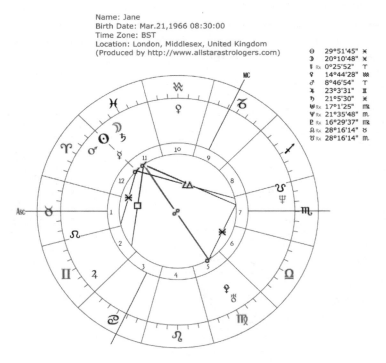

Figure 24: sample birth chart

So if we plot the transiting planets (where they are now) on her birth chart, we see, among other things, that the Sun is in her 4th house. So right now her focus is going to be on home and family. This woman is a friend of mine, and I know that she is on holiday at the moment (which shows up with all the planets transiting her 5th house), with her husband and two kids, which speaks of the family focus.

Take it back to your birth chart

See where the transiting planets are for you.

Using the 'here and now' chart you've just created, showing where the planets are right now (or an ephemeris), work out where all the planets are. Next, plot out where the transiting planets are compared to your birth chart, drawing them in around the outside of the printout of your chart.

What does it all mean?

Once you've plotted in all the transiting planets on your chart, look at their location in terms of which houses they are in. Where is Venus, for example? Let's say transiting Venus is in your 8th house, what could that mean? Look up Venus (see page 55) and look up the 8th house (see page 25) – although the interpretations in this book were written mainly for you to decode your birth chart, you'll still be able to get a sense of what transiting Venus in your 8th house will mean for you.

As you try to decode the transits, remember the following:

❖ **The Sun** acts like a spotlight and moves around your houses over the course of a year. It lights up or focuses on whichever part of the chart it's in. So when it's in your 4th house it's time to focus on family; when it's in the 7th house, it's time to focus on your love life and so on.

❖ **The Moon** shows what you need emotionally.

❖ **Mercur**y shows what's on your mind.

❖ **Venus** shows who and what you're loving.

❖ **Mars** is where you're motivated.

❖ **Jupiter** is where you're lucky.

❖ **Saturn** is where you have lessons to learn.

❖ **Uranus** is where things are evolving.

❖ **Neptune** is where you're inspired or confused.

❖ **Pluto** is where deep and long-lasting transformation is possible and where you need to throw out the dead wood.

Keep these ideas in mind as you see where the planets are today are in your birth chart.

The next step

Next, on your own chart, look at which aspects the transiting planets are making to your natal planets. Is Saturn squaring your Sun? Pluto trining your Venus? Using the keywords in this book, try to work it out. Here's an example:

❖ Saturn (lessons) making things tricky (square) regarding your ego/who you are (Sun).

❖ Powerful influences (Pluto) working in your favour (trine) regarding things to do with love and abundance (Venus).

Then add the layer of the houses; here's an example:

❖ Is transiting Pluto in your 10th house (professional life)? The chances are that what's happening is to do with ongoing themes connected to your career.

❖ Or is Venus in your 4th house? Then the goodness coming your way is likely to manifest connected to 4th house issues such as home and family.

In my friend's birth chart above, one of the biggest things to note is that Pluto is trining her ascendant (transiting planets can make aspects to the planets and angles). In other words, this is the time for her to revolutionize how the world sees her. I don't know how she plans to do this, but in a few months' time, I could well learn that she has somehow transformed her image – perhaps through some kind of dramatic change in her appearance. Or perhaps she will reinvent herself through her job, or in some other way.

If I were reading her chart, I could predict big changes coming up in the way she comes across or in the way she presents herself to the world. Remember, Pluto transforms, trines are harmonious and the ascendant is the way the world sees you or the mask you wear out in the world. So you can expect a positive transformation that reflects this.

Don't worry if all this is not immediately apparent to you. Once you become more familiar with the astrological keywords, it will start to flow. I *highly* recommend Robert Hand's 530-page tome *Planets In Transit*, which is the bible for any astrology student. Mr Hand is my astrological idol, though do be aware that some people find his interpretations a little... intense!

The main thing is to know how to work out where the transiting planets are in your chart, then look to *Planets In Transit* for interpretations that will start to become second nature to you once you've read them often enough. You can also find out (for free) which planets are where for you right now a theastrologybook.com/transits. This is a very simple chart program that simply shows you if the transiting planets are harmonizing or clashing with your birth chart, but it will get you started.

Predicting with planetary cycles

My other favourite way to make easy predictions is to use the monthly New and Full Moons as they go around the chart. You can read all about that technique in my book *Moonology*, which is packed with information about the magical effects of the transiting Moon, but in a nutshell, here's how to do it.

Find out which sign the New Moon is taking place in. This isn't hard to do – you can find it on my website moonology. com, or my Facebook page, Facebook.com/yasminboland. It will also be mentioned by other astrologers on their sites or Facebook pages.

Once you know which sign the New Moon is in, see where (in which house) that falls in your birth chart. Wherever the Moon is new in your chart, you have a restart coming that month, or for the coming six months in the case of a New Moon eclipse. Wherever you have a Full Moon, things are going to come to some kind of release, or you need to let go of someone or something.

Look back at my friend's birth chart above: where does the New Moon in Scorpio fall there? Well, Scorpio rules her 7th house, so a New Moon in Scorpio will bring her new energy related to her love life, her partner, any exes she's still in touch with, her love life in general and, because the 7th house is also about enemies, it could also bring a restart with someone she considers more foe than friend.

And how would the Full Moon in Aries affect this chart? If you look at the chart you'll see Aries rules my friend's 12th house, so a Full Moon in Aries will be about her finding some kind of balance (because Full Moon always asks for balance) between her 6th house (daily work) and her 12th house (spiritual life). It would be a time for her to make sure she was getting enough Zen time to balance out the daily grind. She might be focused (the Sun) on her daily routines and duties (6th house), but she needs to take time out (12th house) to retreat, withdraw and dream (12th house).

Conclusion

As you can now see, astrology is a highly intricate system, and you should be aware that there's still a lot more to learn if you're to become a fully fledged astrologer! There are literally thousands of years of teachings to take in: ancient astrology; Egyptian astrology; Hermetic astrology; Renaissance astrology...

You can learn techniques such as vibration-based astrology, known as harmonics, timing methods such as fidaria and profections, and other forecasting methods such as Solar Returns (a chart set for the moment of your birthday when the Sun is back to the same degree and minute it was when you were born), and so much more. However, you now have a good grounding in the basics of the subject – which is all you need to get started.

Now, please read the book again! I'm serious. There is *so much* to take in. Read it again, alongside your own birth chart and those of your friends and family members. I find that every year I learn something new in astrology, and I revisit birth charts I've seen dozens of times before with fresh ideas.

And if you've skipped great sections of this book and jumped to the Cookbook section, say, I strongly advise you to go back to the beginning and, every time you don't understand something, read it again and then again!

Astrology really builds on itself: you need to fully grasp one concept before you can understand the next. So be patient with yourself and the subject! Also remember that astrology is all about keywords. Learn the keywords and the main ideas of the planets, signs, houses and aspects. With those under your belt, you'll be able to move forwards, deeper and deeper into your studies. Eventually, you may wish to sign up for one of the growing number of workshops, lectures, and even degree courses out there. Or you may prefer to work with one or more mentors.

I would also recommend you sign up for some kind of astrology conference (they are held all over the world) and get yourself as many astrology pals as you can, to share information and ideas (we astrologers are very easily found on the internet!). Fellow newbie astrology students as well as veterans will help you in different ways.

As my first teacher once said to me, quite soon 'you'll see if this is a short-term interest or if it becomes a lifelong passion'. I believe that for me, astrology has been an across-the-lifetimes affair. Maybe it's that for you too?

A final thought: use all the astrological information you discover wisely! It's powerful. Always use it for good. Use it to build people up and make them feel better about themselves. Use it to help people understand their challenges, yes, but also make sure you point out their gifts and advantages as well.

If and when you decide you're ready to give readings, paid or not, you have a massive responsibility to yourself, the person you're reading for and to the subject of astrology itself. Astrology is a tool for self-development and self-empowerment. Use it to know yourself and to help others know themselves.

If you work with predictions, never make anyone feel scared. If you see a big challenge looming on their horizon, explain it in the most uplifting terms that you can. Remind them that lessons usually leave us better off than we were before. Help them to understand what their soul is going through. Remember, we incarnate with the charts that we do for a reason – because our soul wants to learn the lessons of this lifetime, all of which can be found in the birth chart. And we want to go higher. Use astrology to help yourself and other people to feel good. It's a most powerful tool and you need to use it wisely to heal, plan, teach, soothe, explain and assist.

I'm wishing you all the best on your astrological journey!

Stay in touch!

I would love to hear from you and also help you out if you have any queries about this book or if you're struggling with any of the exercises. Here's how to find me:

❖ Via my website, moonology.com

❖ On my two Facebook pages:
 facebook.com/yasminboland
 facebook.com/yasminbolandsmoonology

❖ On Twitter: @yasminboland

❖ On Instagram: @moonologydotcom

Decoding Louise Hay's chart

Read this once you have read the rest of the book!

On page 10 you saw the chart for Hay House founder, Louise Hay. Take another look at the chart and see how the info below matches what you see... and if you can, give yourself a big pat on the back!

❖ Sun in Libra in the 3rd house

❖ Moon in Scorpio in the 4th house

❖ Ascendant in Leo

❖ Mercury in Libra in the 3rd house

❖ Venus in Libra in the 3rd house

❖ Mars in Taurus in the 10th house

❖ Jupiter in Aquarius in the 7th house

❖ Saturn in Scorpio in the 4th house

❖ Uranus in Pisces in the 8th house

❖ Neptune in Leo in the 1st house

❖ Pluto in Cancer in the 12th house

The three closest aspects in Ms Hay's chart are:

1. Mercury conjunct the IC

2. Mars in the 10th square Jupiter in the 7th

3. Sun in the 3rd square Pluto in the 12th

Glossary

Of course, for you, this book is packed with many new concepts and terms – you've learned a whole new way of looking at your life! Hopefully you now feel at home with the new words and phrases you've come across, but here's a very brief overview of some of the astrological terms you might hear about, and wonder what they are.

Classical mythology in astrology

If you go beyond your basic studies, it may interest you to know that there's a lot of Greek and Roman mythology in astrology. Of course, some of the names of the planets are actually Classical gods and goddesses, such as Jupiter and Venus. The more you know about the Greek and Roman references, the better. However, there are so many different ways to study astrology, be it via the myths or in a Jungian fashion or through political astrology. The direction is up to you. But it's worth knowing about the myths. The book *Mythic Astrology* by Liz Greene is a great place to start.

The distance the planets can be from each other

One thing that's good to know when you're starting out is that certain of the faster-moving planets can never be more than a certain distance apart from each other. This might sound more like astronomy, but in astrology it gives you more of a sense of a person. So the Sun and Mercury can never be more than 28 degrees apart, and the Sun and Venus can never be more than 48 degrees apart.

Horary astrology

This is an increasingly popular form of astrology in which you cast a chart for the moment you ask a question – e.g. 'Will my house sale go through?' You then analyse the chart you get using most of the same basic principles employed in natal astrology. It's a fun subject to study and it can be accurate. However, I prefer Tarot cards and Angel oracles.

Intercepted house or sign

I don't use intercepted houses or signs as I use the Whole Sign System. However, this is when you use another house system (such as Placidus or Koch) and one house is bigger than 30 degrees, so you have two signs in it. So say the 4th house starts with one sign in it, has another entire sign in there as well, and then the beginnings of another sign in there afterwards. So you start with one sign – Libra, say – then you get 30 degrees of Scorpio in there and then Sagittarius starts.

Astrologers disagree on the exact meaning of an intercepted house or sign. One theory is that as Scorpio – in this example – doesn't rule a house cusp, you are that bit less Scorpionic than the average person. It may be that you need more Scorpionic energy in your life and for that you would look to working out your Mars or Scorpio. It's also said that where you have an intercepted house or sign in your chart, you should pay special attention to it as it's a bit 'special'.

The midpoint

A midpoint is the point between two planets. They are of interest in the following scenarios: if you have a planet on a midpoint between two of your other planets; if someone else has one of their planets on one of your midpoints; if there is a celestial event (i.e. a New Moon or an eclipse or a planet is transiting) on one of your midpoints. Essentially, the combined energies of the planets triggering and being triggered come to the fore. Some astrologers are crazy about the implications of midpoints, others not so much. If you'd like to learn more, the book to read is Reinhold Ebertin's *Combination of Stellar Influences*.

Mutual reception

This is when one planet is in another planet's sign and vice versa. For example, if Mars is in Taurus and Venus is in Aries.

Returns

You may hear about Saturn Return and other returns once you start to study astrology. This is when a planet returns to where it was on the day you were born. If, say, you were born with Saturn at 18 Aquarius, about 29–30 years after your birth, Saturn will have gone around all the signs (and through all the houses on your chart) and tested you in all those 24 ways (12 sign and 12 houses; Saturn is all about tests). Then Saturn comes back to where he was when you were born.

In the weeks leading up to his return to 18 Aquarius, you are tested further. But you've been tested in every part of your life by now – you're now an astrological grown-up. Moreover, as a result of these tests, you have an idea of what you're made of, how tough you are, what you can withstand, overcome and hopefully learn from. You know how resilient you are. Once Saturn returns to 18 Aquarius, you get to see what in your life is still standing. It's often a time when a person separates more from their parents, because Saturn is about being mature. For what it's worth, I would recommend never marrying anyone until after their first Saturn Return.

Stelliums

A stellium is defined as a group of four, five or more planets all in one sign. It happens more often than you might think. A stellium makes the individual focused on whatever the sign is. So if you have a lot of Aries planets – say your Sun, Moon, Mercury and Venus – then you're 'very Aries' and those planets are called a stellium. For a good introduction to the subject, check out Donna Cunningham's ebook *The Stellium Handbook* (skywriter.wordpress.com).

Synastry

If you go further in your study of astrology, you'll come across this word. It's how astrologers describe the study of astrological compatibility. 'What sort of synastry do you have?' means 'How do your planets fit with his or her planets?'

When you're doing synastry, or compatibility – or looking at how the planets are affecting you now – you're looking at degrees. So in a compatibility chart, for example, you would compare your chart with someone else's, and see whose planets conjoin, trine, sextile, square or oppose whose. Your Venus conjoining, trining or sextiling the other person's Mars (or any other planet) is going to feel much better than his/her Venus, Mars or anything else squaring something in your chart. You need to learn about aspects (see Chapter 8).

Table of dignities

This is a very complicated document that's really beyond the basics of astrology; however, all student astrologers need a table of dignities to hand, so I've included an explanation below. You can also visit theastrologybook.com/dignities for a visual representation of the table.

Essentially, the table of dignities is a guide to which planet rules which part of a sign, once it's broken down into what are called decans. The table of dignities shows which planets rejoice in which sign and which are not so thrilled to be there. Personally, I'm not a huge fan of the table of dignities, yet it's highly regarded by so many people – you can discover what you think of it later. Note that the modern planets aren't included in this table, as it predates their discovery. Below is a brief guide to decoding the table of dignities.

Column 1 shows the signs of the zodiac.

Column 2 shows which planet rules which sign and when (D and N = day and night). For example, Mars rules Aries in the day and Scorpio at night (if you want to look at this on your chart, you'll need to know whether you were born in the daytime or at night). Venus rules Taurus, Mercury rules

Gemini and so on. The planet is at home – in its 'house' – in this sign and feels comfortable.

Column 3 shows which sign each planet is 'exalted' in. That means where it feels best, acts best, fulfils its potential. For example, on the first line the Sun is exalted in Leo. Under that, the Moon is exalted in Taurus. Each planet just has one sign where it's exalted. When the planet is in that sign, it's as though it's an honoured guest. The number shows the exact degree of exaltation – when the planet is there it's extremely strong.*

Column 4 shows the triplicity of the planets: in other words, the planetary rulership of the triplicities. So in the day, for example, the Sun is the triplicity ruler of all the Fire signs. By night it's Jupiter. When a planet is in its triplicity, that placement really suits it. The sign of a planet's triplicity is a familiar, relaxed environment. The planet works well here.

Column 5 shows the terms of the planets. Terms are subsections or sub-rulerships of the signs. The nature of a planet in a sign is altered by the planet in whose term it happens to be. As you can see in the first line of the terms on the table, Jupiter rules 0.0 degrees to 5.59 of Aries, Venus rules 6 degrees to 13.59 degrees of Aries, and so on. For another example, look and you'll see that Jupiter also rules 14 Cancer. When a planet is in its term, it's slightly strengthened.*

Column 6 shows the degrees where rulership by face transfers, also known as the decans. Faces, or decans, are another way to break down the signs. Most astrologers disregard faces and have done for hundreds of years, yet they persistently show up in tables of dignity! When a planet is in its favoured decan, it's slightly strengthened* but not totally comfortable.

Column 7 shows the signs where the planets are in so-called detriment. That means the planet does not do well in this sign. I don't really look at this, as I don't believe that any planet is ever really in trouble in any sign. There is always a positive. Many other modern astrologers agree with me. However, ancient astrologers used detriments and it's a concept worth knowing about.

The detriment of a planet is always the sign opposite the sign it rules. For example, Mars, on the first line, rules Aries, the opposite sign to Aries is Libra and the planet associated with Libra is Venus. When a planet is in detriment, it's at a disadvantage and needs to stick to the rules; it's vulnerable.

Column 8 shows the signs where the planets' experience falls. Again, like detriment, this is not a good thing and again, I don't tend to use it as I've never found it terribly accurate; plus, it's undeniably negative. For the record though, the sign of Fall is the opposite to the sign of a planet's exaltation. When a planet is in its Fall, it has difficulty in expressing itself properly.

* A note on planetary strength and weakness: the stronger a planet is, the more you're likely to feel its influence. And if two planets are making an aspect to each other, the stronger one has stronger control over the outcome of the aspect. For example, if the Moon and Saturn are in trine, they work well together, but if the Moon is strongest, that working well together happens on a more emotional level (Moon).

FAQs

Now let me address some of the questions that may have occurred to you while you were reading the book:

Can I see my life purpose in my chart?
Yes! In your North Node: where is it by sign and house. Read about the Moon's nodes on pages 181–185.

Can I see my past lives in my chart?
Yes: in Saturn and the South Node. If someone has a conjunction from your Saturn to their South Node, or vice versa, it's said to be an unbreakable bond that goes across time and lifetimes. Any strong Saturn connections (especially conjunctions) hint at past lives together. Read about Saturn on pages 61–62 and 217.

My sign doesn't go with my lover's/partner's sign
Don't worry. Look at your Moon, Venus, Mars and Jupiter connections in particular. There is way more to the chart than the Sun sign, as you know by now!

I'm frightened about something in my chart

If you have any worries associated with what you discover in your birth chart, please see a local astrologer or drop me a line via my website, moonology.com – there is nothing to fear!

Do twins have the same birth chart?

As we know, some twins are very alike and some are not. Generally, you'll see that twins who were born within a few minutes of each other and have the same Rising Sign (and thus the same houses and planets layout) are more alike than twins who were born far enough apart for the Rising Sign to have changed. As you know by now, if you have the same planets all set out in different houses, that's going to make a major difference to the way they are expressed.

Should I pick my baby's birth time?

Personally, I wouldn't, but does it really matter, since we're all born at the exact right moment for our soul's needs? So if you choose the time, that's the exact right time. All I can say is good luck with getting it right. In my limited experience of choosing dates, it's hard to find 'the perfect chart'.

When is the best time to get married?

When you want to. The same applies with choosing a date for the wedding. I tested maybe 100 different times and dates for my own wedding, and none of them seemed to be The Ideal. So I closed my eyes and asked the Divine Mother to choose one for me, and a time and date popped into my head. I looked at the chart really briefly and saw Venus was on the MC and went with it. Far better!

Can astrology predict someone's death?

In the olden days, a lot of astrologers would claim to be able to predict their own death. Some may have managed it, but most didn't. Personally, I'm too much of an astrologer-on-the-side-of-the-light to want to peer into such a dark question. Frankly, I'd be a bit wary of any astrologer who offered to do it for you. What's the point? There are some things we don't need to know.

What is a natural chart?

This is a chart that hasn't been cast for anyone or any time in particular. It can be used as an easy and quick reference for the order of the signs, their quadruplicities and triplicities, and which house each sign is naturally associated with. Visit theastrologybook.com/naturalchart to see a natural chart for your reference.

What if I have no planets in a particular house?

You might wonder if not having any planets in a house means nothing will happen to you in that part of your life. However, that is not the case. Where there are a lot of planets in a house, that house is emphasised. However what you need to do with an empty house is take a look at the planet which rules it. For example, if Taurus rules your 8th house, then you would look at the Taurean planet Venus to interpret 8th house matters.

Recommended reading

Below is a list of my favourite astrology books suitable for beginners. All are highly regarded in the field. When it comes to astrology, it's good to know you're reading a title that's considered reputable, so you're not picking up bad habits or strange ideas. All of these books more than pass muster, and they build on what you've learned in this book, in one way or another.

Aspects in Astrology, Sue Tompkins (Destiny Books)

Chart Interpretation Handbook, Stephen Arroyo (CRCS Publications)

Healing Pluto Problems, Donna Cunningham (Red Wheel/ Weiser Books)

Key Words for Astrology, Anna Haebler and Hajo Banzhaf (Weiser Books)

Making the Gods Work for You, Caroline W. Casey (Harmony)

Planets In Transit, Robert Hand (Whitford Press)

Predictive Astrology, The Eagle and the Lark, Bernadette Brady, (Weiser Books)

Spiritual Astrology: A Path to Divine Awakening, Jan Spiller (Touchstone)

Star Crossed, Kim Farnell (lulu.com)

The Astrology Sourcebook, Shirley Soffer (Shirley I. Soffer)

The Changing Sky, Steven Forrest (Seven Paws Press)

The Gods of Change, Howard Sasportas (Penguin Books)

The Inner Sky, Steven Forrest (Seven Paws Press)

The Principles of Astrology, C.E.O. Carter (American Federation of Astrologers)

The Rulership Book, Rex E. Bills (American Federation of Astrologers)

The Twelve Houses, Howard Sasportas (LSA/Flare)

Also see theastrologybook.com for lots more resources to help you on your astrological journey.

Acknowledgements

I feel I could thank every person who has ever helped me (so far) on my astrological journey, but they are legion and that would be a chapter in itself. So instead, I will keep my thanks here to those who made a real difference to this book.

Thank you so much to my fellow astrologer Michelle Pilley and my fellow astrology student Amy Kiberd (yes, I'm an astrologer and yet still an astrology student!), for commissioning this book.

Also very big thanks to Debra Wolter, who doesn't 'do' astrology and yet has managed to edit it, bless her meticulous Mercury in Virgo! And to my unbelievably talented astro-editors, Kelly Surtees and Kim Farnell, who looked at the manuscript at the very beginning and the very end of the writing and editing process. They both encouraged me and added layers of richness with their brilliance.

And finally – last but definitely not least – to Julie Oughton and Moira Boland for their eagle-eyed care and attention to the final manuscript.

ABOUT THE AUTHOR

Yasmin Boland began her career as a freelance journalist with a passion for writing and astrology. Due to various cosmic turns of event, these passions turned into her profession and she is now one of the most widely read astrology writers on the planet, with columns published all over the world.

Yasmin loves pretty much all astrology but has a special interest in the Moon, specifically in New and Full Moons. At her website moonology.com, you can read her Daily Moon Message, plus her weekly, monthly and annual horoscopes; she also has a flourishing Facebook community. Yasmin's previous books include *Moonology* and *Angel Astrology 101* (co-authored with Doreen Virtue). Yasmin was born in Germany, grew up in Tasmania and so far has lived in Australia, France and England.

f yasminboland
yasminbolandsmoonology

y @yasminboland

◉ @moonologydotcom

theastrologybook.com
moonology.com

HAY HOUSE

Look within

Join the conversation about latest products, events, exclusive offers and more.

f Hay House UK

🐦 @HayHouseUK

📷 @hayhouseuk

💜 healyourlife.com

We'd love to hear from you!